EUGENE H. PETERSON

A MONTH OF SUNDAYS

THIRTY-ONE DAYS OF WRESTLING WITH MATTHEW, MARK, LUKE, AND JOHN

WATERBROOK

A Month of Sundays

Hardcover ISBN 978-1-60142-982-7
eBook ISBN 978-1-60142-983-4

Cover design by Kristopher Orr; jacket illustration by Alexey Kurbatov

The author is represented by Alive Literary Agency, Colorado Springs, Colorado, www .aliveliterary.com.

Published in the United States by WaterBrook, an imprint of Random House, a division of Penguin Random House LLC.

WATERBROOK® and its deer colophon are registered trademarks of Penguin Random House LLC.

Library of Congress Cataloging-in-Publication Data:
Names: Peterson, Eugene H., 1932–2018, author.
Title: A month of Sundays : thirty-one days of wrestling with Matthew, Mark, Luke, and John / by Eugene H. Peterson.
Description: First Edition. | Colorado Springs : WaterBrook, 2019.
Identifiers: LCCN 2019012693| ISBN 9781601429827 (hardcover) | ISBN 9781601429834 (electronic)
Subjects: LCSH: Bible. Gospels—Meditations. | Bible. Gospels—Sermons.
Classification: LCC BS2555.54 .P475 2019 | DDC 226/.06—dc23
LC record available at https://lccn.loc.gov/2019012693

Printed in Canada
2019—First Edition

10 9 8 7 6 5 4 3 2 1

SPECIAL SALES
Most WaterBrook books are available at special quantity discounts when purchased in bulk by corporations, organizations, and special-interest groups. Custom imprinting or excerpting can also be done to fit special needs. For information, please email specialmarketscms @penguinrandomhouse.com.

Contents

LUKE

JOHN

Introduction

Eugene Peterson was quite concerned about the language we use between Sundays. He insisted on a continuity of language between the words we use in Bible studies and the words we use when we are out, for example, fishing for rainbow trout. He constantly urged others "to counter the reduction of language to god-talk—language that is severed from a God-created and God-saved world, language that is depersonalized and functionalized. The dreaded god-talk."* Yes, dreaded indeed. Lucky for us, Reverend Peterson led by example not simply between Sundays but on Sundays, too, in his preaching.

We were beyond fortunate to have acquired a considerable chunk of Eugene Peterson's writings, including a portion clearly labeled "sermons." Most of this content reflects his long tenure as pastor of Christ Our King Presbyterian Church in Bel Air, Maryland. Some of this was organized and arranged into one of his last books published before his death—*As Kingfishers Catch Fire.* Some of this content, but not all. What you hold in your hands is a sampling of the "but not all."

A Month of Sundays is exactly that—a Sunday sermon or

---

* Eugene Peterson, "What Are Writers Good For?" (lecture, Tattered Cover, Denver, CO, July 9, 2006).

homily or message or whatever you'd like to call them, for every day of the month, drawn from the four Gospels: Matthew, Mark, Luke, and John. Common sense in the current world of publishing would caution against a collection of sermons, especially thirty-one of them, even if in abbreviated form. Such an offering could easily end up nothing more than a bound bunch of depersonalized and functionalized language. But remember, these are sermons from a man allergic to the dreaded god-talk.

A Month of Sundays is also the title of a work of fiction by author John Updike. His is the story of the Reverend Tom Marshfield, guilty of sexual sins, sent west from his midwestern parish to a desert retreat dedicated to spiritual renewal. As part of his rehabilitation, Marshfield is required to keep a monthlong journal, where he lays bare his soul, his past, and at times his present. Updike's work of fiction and Peterson's bundle of sermons couldn't be further apart. Yet, dedicating thirty-one days to reading and pondering and possibly even journaling around these perspectives on the Gospels could be a form of personal spiritual renewal, maybe even rehabilitation of the soul on some level. After a month of Sundays, it is within the realm of possibilities that you might find yourself in a state of mind similar to Reverend Marshfield's at the conclusion of his stay: "Gratitude is the way He gets us, when we have gnawed off a leg to escape His other snares."*

* John Updike, *A Month of Sundays: A Novel* (New York: Random House, 1975).

Gratitude. A frame of mind and heart far removed from the dreaded god-talk.

Finally, a word about structure. Many of these sermons are spread out over more than one day. When you encounter an opening Scripture passage, that's where things begin. When you arrive, a day or so later, at the word *amen,* that's where the particular reflection ends. This was in an attempt to make the content manageable for a daily reading, and in each case, we believe it did not dilute the strength of the message in any way. In fact, we found each day's portion was, like grace, sufficient. You will also notice a strange rhythm in the first two entries from Matthew—they're short, almost clipped, outline-like. That reflects the documents used to create this collection. In other words, that's what Eugene Peterson's sermon notes reflect. After those two "days," the other entries slow down and take their sweet time. You'll see.

—the WaterBrook Editorial Team

Matthew

Transition

The family tree of Jesus Christ, David's son, Abraham's son:

Abraham had Isaac,

Isaac had Jacob,

Jacob had Judah and his brothers,

Judah had Perez and Zerah (the mother was Tamar),

Perez had Hezron,

Hezron had Aram,

Aram had Amminadab,

Amminadab had Nahshon,

Nahshon had Salmon,

Salmon had Boaz (his mother was Rahab),

Boaz had Obed (Ruth was the mother),

Obed had Jesse,

Jesse had David,

   and David became king.

David had Solomon (Uriah's wife was the mother),
    Solomon had Rehoboam,
    Rehoboam had Abijah,
    Abijah had Asa,
    Asa had Jehoshaphat,
    Jehoshaphat had Joram,
    Joram had Uzziah,
    Uzziah had Jotham,
    Jotham had Ahaz,
    Ahaz had Hezekiah,
    Hezekiah had Manasseh,
    Manasseh had Amon,
    Amon had Josiah,
    Josiah had Jehoiachin and his brothers,
      and then the people were taken into the Babylonian exile.

When the Babylonian exile ended,
    Jeconiah had Shealtiel,
    Shealtiel had Zerubbabel,
    Zerubbabel had Abiud,
    Abiud had Eliakim,
    Eliakim had Azor,
    Azor had Zadok,
    Zadok had Achim,
    Achim had Eliud,

Eliud had Eleazar,
Eleazar had Matthan,
Matthan had Jacob,
Jacob had Joseph, Mary's husband,
    the Mary who gave birth to Jesus,
    the Jesus who was called Christ.

There were fourteen generations from Abraham to David,
    another fourteen from David to the Babylonian exile,
    and yet another fourteen from the Babylonian exile to
        Christ.

MATTHEW 1:1–17

Matthew summarizes close to two thousand years of history, vividly and succinctly, in the opening verses of his gospel. His method is to simply call the roll of significant names. To a people familiar with the names, it was a highly effective method for reviewing a rich history. History, for the gospel writers, was not the scholarly pursuit of determining dates and listing events. It was a personal genealogy, a remembering of their ancestors, God's people.

Matthew arranges the names in three groups, outlining history in three parts.

From Abraham to David (verses 2–6). This is a period of formation. God establishes the nation of Israel in Abraham and the fathers, delivers them from Egyptian bondage in Moses, leads them into a land of promise in Joshua and the Judges, and demonstrates his kingship sovereign rule over them in David.

From David to the deportation to Babylon (verses 6–11). This represents a period of rebellion. God's rule is disputed. The nation becomes divided, the kings fail to demonstrate God's rule, and the people go after other gods. The prophets attempt to call the people back to their origins.

From the deportation to Babylon to the Christ (verses 12–16).
This reflects a period of waiting. The Hebrew people lose their political identity and become people in waiting. They understand
themselves as God's people more accurately, and their expectancy
for the Messiah grows and matures. However, in many ways this is
an obscure and dark time—still, we know enough about it to know
that it was full of intense longing for God's coming again.

So, a question for you. If you could use a time machine to place
yourself back into Hebrew history, which of the three periods
would you choose to live in? Why?

Amen.

Birth

The birth of Jesus took place like this. His mother, Mary, was engaged to be married to Joseph. Before they came to the marriage bed, Joseph discovered she was pregnant. (It was by the Holy Spirit, but he didn't know that.) Joseph, chagrined but noble, determined to take care of things quietly so Mary would not be disgraced.

While he was trying to figure a way out, he had a dream. God's angel spoke in the dream: "Joseph, son of David, don't hesitate to get married. Mary's pregnancy is Spirit-conceived. God's Holy Spirit has made her pregnant. She will bring a son to birth, and when she does, you, Joseph, will name him Jesus—'God saves'—because he will save his people from their sins."

MATTHEW 1:18–21

The birth of Jesus Christ is the nerve center of history, a kind of ganglion that connects all the fibers of mankind's nervous system. His birth brings the past experiences (summarized in Matthew 1:1–17) and the future expectations ("he shall save his people from their sins") into conjunction.

I want to draw your attention to three things:

1. *The fact of the birth.* "[Mary] was found to be with child" (verse 18). There was a real mother and an actual pregnancy. Matthew (and Luke) tells the story in such a way that there is no doubt that it was a physical birth, not a "god-myth." Salvation did not operate outside the process of history.

2. *The manner of the birth.* ". . . found to be with child of the Holy Spirit" (verse 18). God is the initiator and creator of salvation, and Mary's virginity is evidence that God entered history. Salvation was not caused by the processes of history. Incidentally, Joseph's resolve "to divorce her quietly" (verse 19) corroborated Mary's virginity. The first person to believe in the Virgin Birth was not a pious waif but an intelligent skeptic, who knew something about "the birds and the bees."

3. *The meaning of the birth.* "You shall call his name
   Jesus, for he will save his people from their sins" (verse
   21). The birth was not a splendid pageant to brighten
   the long nights of winter or a sentimental myth to
   divert us from the sordid and the dull. It was a ministry that would redeem all creation.

So, a question for you: Why is Christmas an important time to
you personally?

Amen.

Fear

A student doesn't get a better desk than her teacher. A laborer doesn't make more money than his boss. Be content—pleased, even—when you, my students, my harvest hands, get the same treatment I get. If they call me, the Master, "Dungface," what can the workers expect?

Don't be intimidated. Eventually everything is going to be out in the open, and everyone will know how things really are. So don't hesitate to go public now.

Don't be bluffed into silence by the threats of bullies. There's nothing they can do to your soul, your core being. Save your fear for God, who holds your entire life—body and soul—in his hands.

What's the price of a pet canary? Some loose change, right? And God cares what happens to it even more than you do. He pays even greater attention to you, down to the

last detail—even numbering the hairs on your head! So
don't be intimidated by all this bully talk. You're worth
more than a million canaries.

Stand up for me against world opinion and I'll stand up
for you before my Father in heaven. If you turn tail and
run, do you think I'll cover for you?

MATTHEW 10:24–33

They were scared. All twelve of them. You know their names: Peter, Andrew, James, John, Thaddaeus, Bartholomew, Thomas, Philip, Matthew, James the son of Alphaeus, Simon the Canaanite, and Judas Iscariot. Twelve lucky men—lucky to have been called to be with Jesus. And they were scared.

It is odd, really. Puzzling. They had come to realize the most wonderful good news: that God was with them, that God was on their side, and that each of their lives was significant, noticed, valuable, and loved. Everything they had hoped in their deepest hearts might be true, and it even looked like it very much might be true. Being with Jesus had convinced them. And Jesus had called them to accompany him in living out this life and sharing it with the people who didn't know of it.

And now they were scared.

One of my main tasks as your pastor is to keep the image of the Christ-life before you clear and focused and to urge and guide you in its acceptance and practice. I do that in two ways: I tell and then remind you of Jesus's words that bring this life into being, and I listen and understand and pray with you and for you so that it is your lives that are addressed. The underlying conviction of the work of the pastor is that the words of Jesus are as true now as when first spoken, and that every named life in this congregation is as important as those twelve named disciples.

Today I am going back to the story in the middle of Matthew's gospel that shows Jesus first calling the twelve disciples, how they reacted, and how Jesus responded. Jesus called them by name, as he calls us. Every time we baptize an adult or an infant, we recover that glory—that each of us is absolutely unique, chosen for salvation, and infinitely valuable. There is no company or organization that can afford to pay us what we are worth. We are incredibly precious.

But as Jesus continued to talk with them, they realized the dimensions of life that they were being drawn into and began to get nervous. They, in fact, were being called into a fullness and extravagance that they were not used to and were not prepared for. Jesus realized what they were feeling and interrupted their growing apprehension: "So have no fear of them; for nothing is covered that will not be revealed. . . . And do not fear those who kill the body but cannot kill the soul. . . . Fear not, therefore; you are of more value than many sparrows" (Matthew 10:26, 28, 31).

Have no fear. Do not fear. Fear not. Three times Jesus told his twelve disciples not to be afraid.

When we listen, really listen, to the words of Jesus, we know they are for us and that this life has deep, eternal significance. And we are delighted. But we also realize that it is going to demand that we grow up, that we be fully human before God, and that for reasons that we will never quite comprehend, the majority of people around us won't be enthusiastic. We know, deep in our bones, that we are called to be disciples and there is no second-rate person among us. Yet the opposition unnerves us. But Jesus interrupts and says, "Don't be afraid. Don't let what you suppose to be dangerous frighten you. Don't let your minority status bother you. God does not run the world by majority vote. Don't be afraid."

About a year ago, on a clear, blue-sky summer day, my wife, Jan, and I were in a little Piper Cub flying over the Rocky Mountains. We then flew between them, following a river valley, and landed in a remote area called the Bob Marshall Wilderness Area. As we came down out of the skies and approached this meadow, there was no landing strip—just a field of grass, sprinkled with daisies and Indian paintbrushes. I was a little scared. The grass was a foot, maybe a foot and a half, high. There could have been a dead coyote in the grass that we would hit or a large rock or a deep hole. And we were a long way from anyone, with fifty miles of ten-thousand-foot peaks separating us from a hospital emergency room or a mechanic who could repair a crumpled strut.

Norval Hegland was flying the airplane. This red Piper Cub was his plane. We had met Norval and his wife, Margaret, a year ago. Norval is about seventy years old, a retired Norwegian Lutheran pastor with a passion for flying airplanes. He also has a passion for the gospel of Jesus Christ. He was able to combine his two passions by going to Alaska and being the pastor to Eskimo congregations scattered over the northern and western stretches of that gigantic land. There were no roads into those villages and settlements. Norval would fly his plane, often with his wife and three children with him, landing on sandbars in rivers, on the tundra, and on any other clear space he could find. Then he would lead people in worship of God, training and encouraging them to follow Jesus.

Norval has another enthusiasm that amuses me. I don't know if *enthusiasm* is the right word to use with Norval. Norwegian Lutherans don't express a wide range of emotions—at least Norval doesn't. His voice is almost monotone. He doesn't look like the kind of person who would come up with any surprises. But in addition to living and sharing the Christian life and flying airplanes, he is fascinated with filing systems. He files everything and has a complex system that he uses carefully. He likes everything to be in the right place. Margaret, his wife, gets a little tired of it. She says that when he dies, she is going to have his gravestone inscribed with these words: "It's in the file."

Anyway, we are coming down for a landing in this lovely meadow, hoping that Margaret isn't going to have occasion to order that inscription anytime soon. We didn't hit the carcass of a coyote. We bounced along rather pleasantly and came to an easy and safe stop. After tying the plane down, we hiked to a river canyon a few miles away and admired the spectacular results of a million years of river erosion.

There was much to enjoy that day, and we enjoyed it. But there was also much to fear, and we did our share of that. My fear was intermittent—I would see how close we were to the mountain peaks, realize the fragility of the airplane, and have an eruption of panic. But Norval was so relaxed and so experienced. He had been doing this for thirty-five years, flying his wife, children, Eskimos, missionaries, and pastors all over Alaska, North Dakota, and Montana. His confidence and pleasure in sharing all of this wilderness beauty with us was reassuring. But we were still fearful. Jan and I compared feelings later—we both had moments when we were pretty scared. But the fear didn't keep us out of the airplane, and it didn't interfere so much that we weren't able to enjoy the wonder of the day.

The gospel of Jesus Christ is sheer gift. Nothing is more certain than that. It staggers us. It amazes us. It throws us off balance, for we never expected this. But all the same, here it is—the gift of grace. "God so loved the world that he gave" (John 3:16). In the middle of such a grand gift, who can be afraid? Anyone is likely to be. The twelve disciples were. You are. I am. We are. We are afraid that we are in a country that is too large for us, too dangerous. We are afraid that we are not up to it—the love, the suffering, the patient endurance, the opposition. We are afraid that this little Piper Cub of a faith and a church is too fragile to sustain us. We are afraid that our precious egos might crash and become crippled or maybe even die. And our fears close us up—our fears lock the doors and shut the windows of life so that we huddle within ourselves, trying to make our lives snug and safe and predictable.

We are here, in this place, listening to Jesus's words again and realizing our identity as disciples again so that won't happen. So that our fear won't close us in. There is so much to see, so much to experience, so many people to love, such a marvelous Lord to worship. And nothing to fear.

Amen.

Listen

While he was going on like this, babbling,
a light-radiant cloud enveloped them, and
sounding from deep in the cloud a voice:
"This is my Son, marked by my love, focus
of my delight. Listen to him."

MATTHEW 17:5

As I looked at the text for today, I checked my records and discovered I've preached only one sermon from it. I wondered why. But the more I looked at the passage and read and prepared, I knew why. It is one of the most difficult texts in the Gospels to preach from. What do you say about the Transfiguration? What *can* you say? There are some classic responses preachers have made to it, but none of them really struck me as being appropriate here for this congregation. As I was in the process of preparing and finding out what was going on in the passage, a man came into my study and told me something that had just happened to him. When he had finished telling me the story, I thought, *How do you tell the congregation that?* Then he left, and I didn't think anything more about it. I went back to my desk, but his story and this text were stuck together in my mind. In a day or two, the telephone rang, and it was him. He said, "If you're really serious about me telling it, I'll do it."

I'm a pastor. I'm prone to read Scripture, to understand theology, and to talk to you about the history of the church of Jesus Christ. I have one way of coming at things. Many of you have different training. Dr. Bill Maurits is trained as a chemist, not as a theologian. We live in the same world and have the same problems to deal with, but we have different things in our heads and different ways of looking at things. So I've asked Bill to tell you what he told me, and then I am going to try and put the two things together. What I read from this text and what Bill has recently experienced we will hear as the gospel this morning.

> **Bill:** *This is an experience that happened to our family in Atlanta recently. We were driving on one of the superhighways down in the heart of the city in light traffic. I was driving about fifty miles per hour, and we came to a left-hand curve with a vertical bridge abutment just following the road, just a few inches back from the road. I happened to be on the inside of the curve and really couldn't see very much ahead because of the abutment, but I wasn't too concerned. I didn't move out of the lane because I could see the rest of the lanes were moving smoothly and there wasn't much traffic.*
>
> *Well, we got about halfway around the curve and came upon a line of cars absolutely stopped in my lane. I was still going about fifty miles per hour when I finally saw the cars, and I was only about a car length behind the last one ahead of me in line. I figured it up afterward—at fifty miles per hour I was going seventy-three feet per minute, and if you say a nominal eigh-*

teen feet ahead was that "last" car, then I was going to hit him in about a quarter of a second.

In order to do something about that, I couldn't wait that long to turn the wheel a little bit, so I would have had to turn the wheel within one-eighth of a second after I first saw him. Now I don't think, apart from blinking, most people move that fast when they run into surprises, and certainly not after a long fifteen-hour day of driving. I needed something like good luck not to hit him, but there was really no room for good luck this time. I was going faster than I should have been, and I was going to hit him.

I never even got my foot off the accelerator. But here's the thing. We simply smashed into the next lane, and it was about as hard as a bird hitting the window. I don't think the kids in the back seat even realized there was a problem. It all happened so fast that I honestly wouldn't have believed it if I hadn't been rational. But I was, and I'm telling you, all I had a chance to do was watch it happen. I really needed help, and I got it.

I know this loses a lot in translation, and if someone else was up here telling this story, I know what I would be thinking. I'd be thinking, Oh, he wasn't really that close. He probably slowed down a little. But

*I'm telling you what I witnessed. I was there, and the
Lord stepped in and spared my family. I'm just really
thankful.*

Can you see my problem? Can you see how Bill has helped?
You expect me to talk about the intervention of God. But you don't
really expect God to intervene. What I was trying to do as I was
studying this text was find something practical to say to you, because I know that most of you, like Bill, have a scientific education
and are used to looking at the evidence. I don't want to be irrelevant
to that world, so when I come upon a text in the Bible about three
men in the high mountains seeing a vision, I don't want to get too
far away from you. I want to find something down to earth to say,
something you can grab hold of and go home and try out. As I was
doing that kind of thinking, Bill comes in and tells me about a
miracle. He didn't use the word *God* as he told me the story, but the
inference all the way through was that God provided. He and his
family were preserved by the grace of God.

I admit to feeling a little embarrassed because there I was, the
pastor who was supposed to be talking about God but was trying
to talk about men, and Bill, who works with all things practical,
comes in and tells me about God. We need one another, don't we?
The task of preaching involves this kind of intercession, where together we hear the Word of God that comes down to us and we

find it in a place in our lives where it makes a difference. And we sacrifice neither the supernatural nor the natural as we do it.

The mountain of Transfiguration is one of those places where such a connection is made. It takes the experiences of ecstasy, of hearing God speak and seeing God do something out of the ordinary in such a convincing way that you can't leave it behind. It goes with you and stays with you. Here were the disciples of Jesus. They had been walking together for years, and Peter had just made his confession: "You are the Christ, the Son of the living God" (Matthew 16:16). Jesus then took them to the high mountain where they saw a vision and heard the words: "This is my beloved Son . . . ; listen to him" (17:5). How do you tell a story like that—a private experience that is pretty much unbelievable? The same way Bill told his story. You gather together, just like we are this morning, and you make a public proclamation so that we in turn, when and if something similar happens to us, are able to do the same thing. Such things aren't easily talked about in the marketplace, so to speak. But this isn't the marketplace. This is the church, the gathering of the people of God, the God who seems to enjoy doing things beyond what we can sometimes imagine.

When Peter, James, and John saw Jesus transfigured before their eyes, they saw him in a way more glorious than they had previously. The Greek word for what happened is our English word *metamorphosis*—"changed, transformed." The reality on that day on that mountain was that the inside got outside, and those three men saw it. In a very real way, they were changed as well, at least in the way they understood reality from that moment on. Paul used that same language when he wrote, "Do not be conformed to this world but be transformed" (Romans 12:2). There it is—that same word from the Transfiguration. There are things that happen in our lives, things we witness that from a worldly perspective are simply unbelievable. But we are to be transformed—changed in our thinking and seeing and living. We are to be witnesses, just like Peter and James and John and Bill, to all we've seen and heard.

Amen.

Mark

Day 5

Beginning

The good news of Jesus Christ—
the Message!—begins here.

MARK 1:1

In anything of importance, the beginning is crucial. There is probably not a person here who would deny that in coming to Christ's life, we are approaching the most important area of existence, and that which underlies all of our lives and their many activities. If that is not true, then we are engaged in an utter illusion. Three things are important in making a success of this beginning: the vocabulary we use, the mental frame of mind we are in, and the place where we start.

These three are important in nearly any beginning. The vocabulary used determines our capacity to understand what is ahead. And it isn't simply a matter of knowing a word's dictionary meaning but of having sufficient experience using it. One of the problems of youth is that they haven't sufficient experience with words to know what they mean, and as a result they are frequently engaged in confusion, misunderstanding, and despair. What does, for instance, *I love you* mean? A dictionary isn't going to help.

The mental frame of mind is also of primary importance at the beginning. Regardless of what the objective content is, if the mental approach to it is faulty, it cannot be perceived or grasped. We would rather stand watching Niagara Falls with a poet who heard in its thunder a prophet's voice and saw in its leaping rainbows angel's vestments than with the mythical Texan who is reported to have said he knew a plumber who could fix it.

And the place where we begin is important. If we begin with the wrong perspective, we will never be able to get to certain goals. You may remember the story of the six blind men of India who were confronted with an elephant and asked to describe him. They all started in a different place. One grabbed his trunk and said he was like a giant snake. The second ran into the two front legs and said he was like a forest. The third got a ladder and ascended the side, observing that it was a massive impenetrable wall. The fourth, grabbing hold of the tail, proclaimed him to be a ropelike creature. The fifth, tangled up under the belly and within the four legs, announced him to be a kind of cave. And the sixth, feeling the large ear, described him as a sheet of rubber. They were all a little bit right but, more than anything else, all decisively wrong.

Conveniently, we have at hand a couple hundred years of recent history of faulty beginnings in coming to the life of Christ, and the mistakes some men have made may benefit us. Men have come to the life of Christ and, ignoring the necessity for a correct beginning in vocabulary, mental attitude, and place, have begun from their own selves. They've pushed him through their own small minds until what came out, while always having elements of truth to it, was always a great deal more wrong than right. Jesus emerged in novels and literary studies as a social revolutionist, an ethical pioneer, a proclaimer of the end of the world, the world's best salesman, a gentle friend and storyteller to little children, a rustic, rough fisherman most characteristically himself on the storm-tossed Galilean lake with his cronies, a romantic religious leader, a Freudian mystic, the first Communist, the first Nazi, and just about anything else you can think of.

This kind of thing began in the early 1700s under the heading of the writing of Lives of Jesus, but it was called to a halt finally by a young theologian in Germany with a monumental and devastating book, *The Quest of the Historical Jesus*. He showed that attempts to write the history of Jesus were nine-tenths propaganda and one-tenth uncertain history. There wasn't enough history to make a book out of it, and to fill in the gaps and make a book long enough to be respectable, interpretation and imagination were woven in. He showed that it was quite impossible to write a history of the life of Jesus, for all we really had was a faint Galilean figure standing on the shores of a lake, who had gotten himself killed by the Romans, probably foolishly and needlessly. In that skepticism and despair, the young theologian gave up theology and the study of the life of Jesus, thinking it a difficult job, and went off to Africa to serve as a medical doctor. He is famous to us now as the great humanitarian Albert Schweitzer.

That is the history and the fate of attempts to write a life of Jesus. It doesn't sound too promising for us as we look at his life and assess its value for ourselves. So what do we do? Well, first of all, we make a different beginning. We won't write a life of Jesus. But we still have to do something with it.

We have assumed his name as Christians. We have made specific promises of discipleship as members of his church. We are on several counts involved in a practical daily response to his life. The life of Christ has practical importance for each of us, but our part in assessing and assimilating that importance contains the same dangers that have been indicated in this episode of the literary and theological life of Jesus. We are in danger on the one hand of using the name of Jesus as a pretense for living any kind of life we happen to prefer—that is, using the Christian part of our lives as front propaganda and filling in all the details on our own. On the other hand, we are in danger of real skepticism—doubting the real, relevant historicity of Jesus's life and finding little in it of practical value for us, who live with families, work, and tensions in a busy technological world that has vastly changed since the first century. We are in danger here of doing what Schweitzer did—leaving the whole business and going our own way and doing the best we can by our own lights.

Day 6

Gospel

A wrong beginning here can derail the whole thing and result in complete failure to discover and live out anything authentic and realistic in Christ's life. So it is especially important that we begin our look at the life of Jesus carefully. Our task is easier because we are following Mark, and Mark made a careful beginning. Mark began with a special vocabulary, with a special mental frame of mind, and in a special place. These three stand at the threshold of the life of Christ, with good reason.

The special vocabulary is discernable in the first sentence: "The beginning of the gospel of Jesus Christ . . ." (Mark 1:1). The important word here is *gospel*. It is an old word, both in the Jewish and pagan worlds. It meant the publication of good news. But it was not just any good news that might be found in the headlines of a newspaper. It was specifically in regard to the kingdom, to some aspect of the rule of the king. It was the glad news to the populace, resulting from some statement or action of their king. This word, used before anything is said at all, defines the contents of Mark's book as primarily information (that can anticipate a glad reception) about the reign of Jesus Christ.

The use of the word suggests that the story is written from the point of view of a man who knows how it turns out—that is, from the point of view of the Resurrection. Mark was a believer, one who had participated in the fellowship of the early church, who knew the power and presence of the risen Christ. As he wrote this account of Jesus, he would naturally be most of all a preacher, telling things that showed Jesus as the ruling King of our lives in his characteristic activity—activity that was practical and relevant for everyone.

So we have no dates, no information about his birth and childhood, and no information on the political, social, or family situation. These are all things that we think are very important in biographies written today. But then Mark was not writing a life but was proclaiming a gospel—the good news of the reign of God—and so he put down the things that were relevant for that. And that means when we look at the life of Jesus, we will not find an ideal life we can imitate but a Master and King we can obey.

Gospel is the word Mark began with, and the mental frame of mind was provided by John the Baptist. In all the Gospels, John the Baptist had the definitive part to play in opening the public ministry of Jesus. According to all traditions, he stood in the light of God's redemptive plan right from the beginning. He himself was part of the gospel of Jesus Christ.

John provided the special mind-set—that necessary frame of mind—by calling men to repentance. Repentance meant that a man should reverse directions, change the mode of life to which he had become accustomed, and reorient himself. Repentance meant the opening up of a new horizon not previously visible. It extended further and comprised more than the individual renewal of man in his inner life. *About face!* That meant make room here in our present existence for the coming world change.

The gospel of Christ was not, you see, just another addition to man's already full and busy life. It was not just another way of looking at things or a few new commandments or another especially heroic example to admire and perhaps follow. The gospel of Christ was good news, but good news about a new kingdom. And kingdoms by definition are exclusive. You can't have two of them in the same place at the same time. Repentance was the preparatory action for this new rule. It was throwing out one kingdom in preparation for the advent of another. It was the tearing down of the slum tenements so the new buildings full of air and light could be constructed.

The gospel of Christ, in other words, is not something we can survey like the goods in a department store, picking and choosing articles from it we like. It is all one parcel—it is the breaking in of a kingdom of absolute rule and government. The only way we can receive it is by turning away from all that has previously been occupying us and taking it in entirely.

John the Baptist is responsible for providing this mental reversal so that we might truly apprehend Christ. And that is why the church, far from merely assigning to [John] a temporal and now accomplished task . . . recognised him to be the one who will be for ever preparing the way for Christ and who, so to speak, stands guard at the frontier of the aeons [our lives]. The way to Christ and into the kingdom of God did not merely at one time—in a moment of past history—lead through John the Baptist, but it leads once and for all only along that path of repentance shown by him. Faith in Jesus Christ is only there where the believer, for himself and within himself, lets the shift of the aeons [realms of living] take place in his own life.*

---

* Günther Bornkamm, *Jesus of Nazareth,* trans. Irene and Fraser McLuskey and James M. Robinson (Minneapolis: Fortress, 1995), 51.

Day 7

Desert

The desert is the place where this word (gospel) is announced and this special frame of mind (repentance) is cultivated. "Since ancient times the desert is the place with which Israel's expectations of the end were associated; for it is an ancient belief that the end shall be as the beginning."*

Thomas Merton says this about the desert:

The Desert Fathers believed that the wilderness had been created as supremely valuable in the eyes of God precisely because it had no value to men. The wasteland was the land that could never be wasted by men because it offered them nothing. There was nothing to attract them. There was nothing to exploit. The desert was the region in which the Chosen People had wandered for forty years, cared for by God alone. They could have reached the Promised Land in a few months if they had travelled directly to it. God's plan was that they should learn to love Him in the wilderness and that they should always look back upon

* Günther Bornkamm, *Jesus of Nazareth,* trans. Irene and Fraser McLuskey and James M. Robinson (Minneapolis: Fortress, 1995), 45.

the time in the desert as the idyllic time of their life with Him alone.*

Mark portrayed John beginning his ministry in the desert, calling men to repentance, and he portrayed Jesus beginning his ministry in the desert, enduring forty days of temptation. The gospel finds its genesis in the desert—the place of wasteland, the region of quietness, where all temptations are overcome, where the outside world can provide no distraction. Where God is most free to speak to the soul.

If the new word, *gospel,* is the vocabulary by which we learn of the dawn of God's kingdom, and if repentance is the act of will and the new mind-set whereby we become open and free to accept the new rule of God breaking into our lives, then the desert is the place where we do it. The desert is a sign of our poverty and the world's emptiness. It's a symbol of our nakedness before God and our willingness to leave all and follow him.

When we wish to read a good book and immerse ourselves in it, we do not go to a noisy bus station to read. Rather, we retreat to a quiet, private place to give ourselves completely to the book. When we wish to talk with someone who means much to us, we take him or her to a place where there will be no interruptions.

---

* Thomas Merton, *Thoughts in Solitude* (New York: Farrar, Straus, and Giroux, 1958), 4–5.

When we study for an examination, we lock the door, turn off the radio, and give ourselves unreservedly to the subject matter. When we want to let the life of Christ make a revolutionary impact on our life, we go to the desert.

Geographically it is not always possible. But we can do it spiritually by recognizing the terrible distraction of the ambitions, the standards, the music, the talk, and the noise of this world to our attempts at spiritual concentration—and then do something about it. The desert we begin in will have to be one of our own making, but it can be made. Some people fast to remind themselves that the bread of this world is not the primary nourishment of their lives. Some people make sacrificial, disciplined acts to train themselves in a mental and emotional way for the spiritual lives they profess.

In our church there is no coercion and no legislation in such matters, but we have the clear witness of Mark that the gospel begins in the desert. It is a place to sharpen goals and renew perspectives. In the clearer, cleaner air of obedience and discipline, we can see His life impinging on ours. "Sky is less changed than earth by altitude."* We see the emptiness of all the world and the fullness of the reign of God.

By beginning with this new word (gospel), this new frame of mind (repentance), and this place (the desert), the life of Christ will

---

* Edith Lovejoy Pierce

reach deeply into our lives and form us as new creations. The beginning is so important. There are no shortcuts. And really, everything is at stake here. For the reign of God is here already in Jesus Christ and ready to break into our lives.

Amen.

Repent

John the Baptizer appeared in the wild,
preaching a baptism of life-change that
leads to forgiveness of sins.

MARK 1:4

Have you seen those greeting cards that are fairly popular today? They have as a legend "Repent and be saved." There is an asterisk after the word *repent* that refers to a footnote, and the footnote says, "If you have already repented, disregard this notice." Well, if you have already repented, you can disregard this sermon. Because that is what it is about. But don't go away yet, because I want to make sure that you and I both understand the same thing about repentance. Then about halfway through, if you've satisfied yourself that you have repented, you can leave. It's legitimate in about ten minutes to walk out. There'll be an usher at the door to receive your offering.

There is an interesting history of the word *repentance*. The word in Hebrew means originally "to take a deep breath and sigh." A deep feeling of sorrow, of remorse. Repentance at the root, at the very beginning, seems to have the idea that you realize that you have done something wrong and you feel badly about it. And you feel it deeply; it gets down deep inside you, and you groan or sigh or you breathe deeply. All of us know how that works. We know that part of repentance. We know the part that has to do with our feelings.

The interesting thing is that use of the word didn't last long in the Bible. Very quickly the writers began to substitute another word for the same action, and this other word meant "return" or "turn around and go." Not a word of feeling at all, but a word of action. Under the influence of the prophets, repentance became not something you felt but something you did. And it's essential you get that through your head if you are going to understand what the Bible means about repentance. You don't repent by taking a deep breath and then feel better. You repent only when you turn around and go back or toward God. It doesn't make any difference how you feel. You can have the feeling, or you don't have to have the feeling. What's essential is that you do something. The call to repentance is not a call to feel the remorse of your sins. It's a call to turn around so that God can do something about them.

John the Baptist was called the forerunner of our Lord. He prepared the way. He got people ready to listen and respond to Jesus Christ. And the way he did it was to preach repentance. That's pretty much all he talked about. That's all we know he talked about. A baptism of repentance. Now, remember he's not calling the people together and playing on their emotions by saying, "What terrible people you've been. Don't you feel badly for the way you've lived? Shed a few tears." He didn't do that. He used a word that by John's time in history had an action meaning. He was saying, "Turn around. Start looking in a different direction. Start going a different direction. God's coming to you. Get ready for it."

There is an old story around the Ozarks about a fiddler who always played just one note on his fiddle, and someone came up to him one day and said, "Zeke, all these other fiddlers play a lot of different notes. How come you just play one note?" He replied, "Well, all those other guys are looking for the right note. I've found it." And that's the impression you get with John the Baptist. He had one note he played, and he kept playing it and playing it and playing it.

A lot of other people were saying a lot of other things about the coming of the Messiah. Some of them were a lot more interesting, but John just kept plunking away, "Repent, repent, repent." Because, you see, John knew that there is really not a whole lot we can do about our salvation. God has done all that needs to be done. God has prepared a life for us and a salvation for us, which is fantastic. It's complex. It's intricate. It's wonderful. And there's not much we can contribute. In fact, you might say that there is not anything we can contribute. But there is something we have to do. We have to turn around.

We have to go that way. We have to open ourselves up to that direction. And so, the monotony of the word *repent,* the singleness of John's message, didn't get complicated with us. He didn't get fancy, and he didn't have complicated doctrines he tried to get us to understand. He just wanted to get us to turn around so that we are there for God to do something with us in Jesus Christ.

Day 9

Happy

N ow there's an important element in this repentance that can be traced back to Isaiah, the Old Testament prophet, which also becomes part of John's message. There's a kind of anticipation to this repentance that is cheerful. I don't know what kind of picture you have of John the Baptist, but the stereotype is a kind of dour, gloomy, even angry man.

When we see the word *repent,* the cartoons always have a kind of angry look on the person who says it, such as someone carrying a placard saying that the end of the world is coming: "Repent. Things are going to get a lot worse if you don't. Repent or doom is going to strike." So in popular language the word *repent* often gets all that kind of stuff thrown into it, but that didn't come from the Bible. It didn't come out of the gospel, because John talked about the forgiveness of sin when he talked about repentance. And that's a happy thing. John's message of repentance was for the forgiveness of sins—getting you ready for the forgiveness of your sins, making it possible for God to do his work in you. And so, the word *repent* in John's tone and context opens you toward joy, breaks you loose toward expectation, and sensitizes you to something cheerful and happy. I very much imagine that John, when he was talking about repentance, was doing it with some jubilation in his voice. He saw something good coming. He said the hard word in order that the people could hear the good word.

It reminds me of what I observe in the days leading up to Christmas. One of the things I've noticed is the terrific amount of anger that is expressed in shopping centers and stores. Do you notice how angry people get with their kids when they're shopping? They jerk 'em and yell at 'em, and they're mad most of the time. This is very odd when you begin to think about it because presumably what people are shopping for is something joyful. They are preparing for a feast, a happy time, a holiday. And yet the elements that go into doing that provoke a lot of irritation. Now, I know that none of you do that. I know that when you are in shopping centers, you're imperturbable. But when you're there, look around you to see the other people who get angry, and wonder why they do. I wonder if one of the reasons they do is because they are wrongheaded about their preparations. They are trying to get ready for a joyful event without doing the preparatory work needed to participate in joy.

You see, most of us have things wrong in our lives. I'd even go so far as to say all of us have things wrong in our lives. We have areas where we are not quite right with God and are not obeying him the way we should. We have relationships with people around us that aren't quite as ardent and pure as they ought to be. We're sinners, in fact, and we carry that legacy of sin with us day after day. If we don't do anything about it, it accumulates and builds. And if we start looking for fuller lives and try to get by just adding things on to what we are doing, it doesn't work. It is like building a beautiful house on a lousy foundation.

The only way to prepare for the good life, for the joyful life, is to do something basic about what's gone wrong with us before. We need to repent, which means asking for forgiveness and getting back to those basic essentials between you and God and between you and others. Restore what needs to be restored. Ask for forgiveness where needed so that we can go on and share the gift. Our inability or our unwillingness to do that is, I'm sure, what produces a lot of our "dis-ease." A symptom, perhaps, yet it's also evidence of our frantic attempts to grasp for joy, to share joy, and to give joy to others instead of first going back and doing that basic homework of the heart that is central to our lives, where we forgive and are forgiven and where we find God's love and then learn how to share it. Hard preparation produces easy enjoyment. And if we slack on the preparation, the enjoyment is going to be superficial and shallow.

Amen.

Start

John the Baptizer appeared in the wild, preaching a baptism of life-change that leads to forgiveness of sins. People thronged to him from Judea and Jerusalem and, as they confessed their sins, were baptized by him in the Jordan River into a changed life. John wore a camel-hair habit, tied at the waist with a leather belt. He ate locusts and wild field honey.

As he preached he said, "The real action comes next: The star in this drama, to whom I'm a mere stagehand, will change your life. I'm baptizing you here in the river, turning your old life in for a kingdom life. His baptism— a holy baptism by the Holy Spirit—will change you from the inside out."

At this time, Jesus came from Nazareth in Galilee and was baptized by John in the Jordan. The moment he came out of the water, he saw the sky split open and God's Spirit, looking like a dove, come down on him. Along with the Spirit, a voice: "You are my Son, chosen and marked by my love, pride of my life."

MARK 1:4–11

Life is complex, exceedingly complex. The moment we wake up to what is involved in being human beings, we very often feel like we are in the middle of a labyrinth. We try this passage and end up at a dead end, and then this one, and then that one. We ask for directions and are given bad ones.

Just about the time we get the animal skills mastered—learn to walk, to eat with a spoon and fork, get toilet trained, acquire enough language so that we can understand the natives—we find that there is a lot more to it, that being a higher form of animal is not enough. We have to be human, and we don't know the first thing about it.

That is why adolescence is such a messy time: we are trying to find our way in a world that we don't know much about. We know our address, that's true, and can find our way home after dark. We know our vocabulary lists and can make ourselves understood to strangers. We know how to count and can figure out how to pay for a Big Mac and french fries and get the right amount of change back. But being human—being me—how do I go about doing that?

But this messiness is not confined to adolescence. We are pushed or fall into it over and over throughout our lives. Things deteriorate into chaos, and we have to start all over again. So where do we start?

We start with the baptism of Jesus. We go to the river and look and listen. We stand on the edge of the Jordan River and watch John the Baptist take the hand of his cousin, Jesus of Nazareth, let him walk out to a depth of three or four feet in the river, and baptize him, immersing him in those waters and then lifting him out again, drenched and clean and alive. We observe what happens, and we listen to what is said. And we say, "That looks like a good start. I think I'll start there too."

This, of course, is not the origin of life. A beginning has already been made. And we ourselves had a beginning that precedes any self-awareness of beginning—we were conceived and born and experienced many wonderful things (and some not so wonderful) that were formative for us but that we will never remember.

But there is a point at which we become self-aware, conscious, and awake to the world and realize that we are actors and creators and have something to say about our lives and something to do that might be significant. Life is not simply being done to us, but we have an agency and we ourselves are alive and matter. It is the time that, in the language of the church, we discover we have not only a body and mind but also a soul. And the soul is full of energy and bursting with curiosity and adventure—we are ready to really live now.

Annie Dillard wrote a wonderful book titled *An American*

Childhood about this moment of waking up to life. She wrote of the surprise of finding yourself awake in a world of insects and rocks and parents and friends—and then the bewilderment of getting in your own way and finding that you are stumbling all over yourself in this wonderful world and wondering where to make a good start.

The Christian answer to this experience is baptism. Baptism is where we make a good start. For this is where Jesus made a good start.

Day 11

Start by...

Trusting our ancestors
(Jesus was baptized by John.)

Jesus didn't baptize himself. John was in a direct line from the prophets—those men and women who kept God's Word alive in the community of God's people. Jesus volitionally entered that stream of the past, accepted its truths, and became a companion to his ancestors. For all his originality and all his uniqueness, Jesus did not begin a new religion. His life did not begin something new but fulfilled something old.

Any true beginning or any good start is this way. None of us, not even Jesus, knows enough to start off on our own.

We start with what is given to us—the language, the food, the music, the clothes that have been handed to us. Later on, if we wish, we can modify or change these gifts, but we begin with trust and in trust. We receive from our ancestors in the faith the stories of faith and the places and times of worship. And that means that we don't have to begin full of anxiety and worry. We can begin relaxed.

The life in Christ is unique—you are not fitting into someone else's mold, meeting anyone's expectations, or trying to conform to a model. You will become more yourself and less like anyone else in the whole world as you do this. But you begin by trusting your ancestors in the faith.

Listening to God
(There was a voice from heaven.)

God speaks. At his baptism, Jesus heard God speak to him. The general and universal speech of God is addressed and personalized in the event of baptism. The wonderful and profound "For God so loved the world" (John 3:16) that is at the heart of the Christian faith becomes "For God so loved Michael and Susan and James and Deborah."

We make a good start when we listen to God speak to us. This requires attentiveness and concentration. God does not speak in competition with other speakers, so he does not raise his voice or hire an advertising agency or public relations firm to work out a strategy to get us to listen. Because he speaks in his own voice, not in imitation of voices that we are more used to, many people never hear him. But he speaks all the same.

Listen to him speak in the sacraments. Listen to him speak in Scripture and sermons. Listen to him speak in the quietness and silence. Listen to him speak in and under and around the voices of friends, family members, poets, singers, and storytellers.

There is no trick to this, no magic, and no spiritual hocus-pocus. There is only attentiveness and a determination that is not easily discouraged to say, "What God says to me is more important than what anyone else ever says. I am going to listen and listen and listen, and I am going to hear. I am going to put myself in the place of listening—in worship, before Scripture, and with listening friends."

Embracing God's affirmation
("With you I am well pleased.")

You make a good start by embracing God's affirmation of you. The first words Jesus heard were "Thou art my beloved Son; with thee I am well pleased" (Mark 1:11). What is basic for Jesus is basic for us, and we can make a good start only if we begin with the right words: the words are from God, and they are "With you I am well pleased."

This affirmation is not self-evident. Many other people have said things quite different from this, and some of them have been the exact opposite: "With you I am not at all well pleased," "With you I have some hopes, but only if you shape up considerably will I ever be well pleased with you," or "I might be well pleased with you if you quit doing this and start doing that."

We are not affirmed by the people around us but are blamed and rebuked and bribed. And the reason, of course, is that in the eyes of the people around us, we need quite a lot of fixing up before we are satisfactory. But God affirms us just as we are. He accepts us without condition. This is a great mystery, and we have difficulty handling it. But it is the gospel of Jesus Christ. God's affirmation doesn't condone our sin, and it doesn't acquiesce in our mediocrity. He calls us to repentance and holiness and discipleship. But he begins with a simple, unconditional affirmation: *I love you. You are my daughter. You are my son. With you I am well pleased.*

When we embrace that affirmation, we make a good start. We don't start falteringly, hesitantly, guiltily, waiting for rejection, or wondering when we will get cut from the squad. We start on the right foot, embraced and embracing the God who loves us and has an eternal salvation for us.

We start with the baptism of Jesus. We go to the river and look and listen. And we observe and we say, "That looks like a good start. I think I'll start there too, trusting my ancestors in the faith, listening to God, and embracing God's affirmation of my life."

Amen.

Tempted

At once, this same Spirit pushed Jesus out into
the wild. For forty wilderness days and nights
he was tested by Satan. Wild animals were his
companions, and angels took care of him.

MARK 1:12–13

Three things happen in rapid sequence: Jesus is baptized, he is tempted, and he begins his public ministry. The baptism is the event that marks Jesus as God's beloved Son, as the Spirit descends upon him, anointing him with the power of God. The ministry Jesus exhibits in the world ministering to people in all their needs, capable and compassionate, able to go directly to the center of what needs to be done and then doing it. The temptation links the two together.

Jesus does not proceed directly from his baptism to his ministry. Mark makes sure we understand that. Sandwiched between these two more glorious, more public events, the temptation is made to seem even more important. We need to know why it is there and what it means.

The Holy Spirit is behind the temptation incident, which is to say that God is behind it. It is not an unfortunate interlude, not a freak interruption of a smoothly planned strategy. The same Holy Spirit that descends upon Jesus at his baptism and later empowers him to preach and heal, here drives him out into the wilderness. A strong word—*pushed*. When we read it we know that there is a quality of necessity about the temptation. This is not a gentle nudge, not a "still small voice" advising the conscience. This is a relentless push.

Whatever else the temptation is, it is not an option. It is not something Jesus can choose to do or not do. If there is going to be any connection between baptism and ministry, there must be temptation. Or to speak of ourselves, if there is going to be a connection between who we are and what we do, there must be something like temptation to link them. This is why we need to understand the meaning of Jesus's testing or there will be a void in our lives between who we feel ourselves to be and what we spend most of our time doing.

We are not to think of the wilderness as a bad place, an empty place, or a desolate place. It was empty enough of vegetation and human artifacts. But it was full of God, packed with the associations of God's great acts of salvation and preservation. In the wilderness, Jesus was with the wild beasts, and the angels ministered to him. It is a description somewhat reminiscent of Eden, as wild animals are unspoiled by man's domestic drudgery. We are in the context of God's creation, a creation full of life typified by the wild beasts. We are also aware of the rarefied atmosphere in which God relates directly to man. The angels are servants of God, ministering to the needs of man. There is a return to that original, uninterrupted, unspoiled community of spiritual beings. If the wild beasts represent the entire order of natural creation, seething with a kind of raw beauty and innocent energy, the angels keep us in touch with the infinitely complex and diversified community that constitutes divine fellowship.

But what happened there in that wilderness of wild animals and angels? The action is described in a phrase: "tempted by Satan" (Mark 1:13). However glorious the wilderness might sound, the word *Satan* throws an ominous wrench in things. There is now an intruder, one who could as easily corrupt the wilderness as he had the Garden of Eden. *Tempt* is a word with a double meaning. It means "test," and it also means "seduce." It can mean either one, or it can mean both at once. *Testing* refers to everyday experiences. We test airplanes to find out if they are safe for passengers. We test fishing lines to see if they will hold big fish. We test medicines to know whether they will heal or harm. When something important is at stake, we like to have a testing beforehand. When David was going forth to meet Goliath, he was loaded down with King Saul's magnificent armor. David, who had never worn anything but a shepherd's cloak, took it off and said, "I can't go with these weapons because I have not tested them." (See 1 Samuel 17:39.) David had no experience with them and therefore would not risk them in such an important battle. Testing is something we do not want to omit from life. If there is no testing, there will be no certainty, no confidence.

But the word also means "seduce" or "test with hostile intent" or "pressure in order to ruin." This is the meaning we ordinarily, in English, give the word *tempt*. It is a testing that is motivated by the

wish that we should fail. No one objects greatly to being tested, for
even if the process is arduous, the results are useful. But we don't
welcome temptation, for by it we are subjected to negative pressures. The person who tests us wants to make us better. The person
who tempts us wants to make us worse.

Jesus experienced both aspects. He was pushed into the wilderness by God in order to be tested. And while he was there, he en-
countered Satan, who tempted him. This combination intensified
the experience. It was an ordeal. The writer to the Hebrews com-
mented on this episode by saying, "We have not a high priest who
is unable to sympathize with our weaknesses, but one who in every
respect has been tempted as we are, yet without sin. Let us then
with confidence draw near to the throne of grace, that we may receive mercy and find grace to help in time of need" (Hebrews
4:15–16).

The testing-temptation focuses a decision for or against God.
What was on trial was Jesus's readiness to commit himself wholly
to God—to in fact be in public what his baptism had proclaimed
him to be in private and to be for others what God had told him he
was to him. Jesus was in the wilderness for forty days. According to
ancient doctors, this is the length of time it takes for an embryo to
mature to the point where it makes its first movements and has
discernable form. Often in the Greek world, men had to be at least
forty years old to take on important jobs, such as a lawgiver. The
disciple of a rabbi had to be forty years old to make independent

decisions. Moses was on Mount Sinai for forty days being instructed in the Law, even while the people of Israel were forty years in the wilderness maturing as the people of God.

The forty days then is a concentration of growth that produces maturity. Jesus moved from his baptism, the Messiah in embryo, through the forty-day period of temptation and came out the other side as the complete man (the "Son of God") equipped to be God's Messiah and inaugurate the rule of God's kingdom. Temptation—the kind that Jesus experienced and the kind that is a necessity in our lives—is a kind of adolescence of the spirit. A time of testing to find out what works for us. A time of intensified experience in which we find the personal meaning of what God tells us about ourselves. No part of the gospel is just information or a mere idea. It is all here to be experienced by faith and used in the service of God for others.

Amen.

Luke

Day 13

Geography

He came to Nazareth where he had been reared.
As he always did on the Sabbath, he went to the
meeting place. When he stood up to read, he
was handed the scroll of the prophet Isaiah.

LUKE 4:16–17

The Christian life is physical. It is also spiritual. There are prayers to be said, praises to be sung, ideas to be comprehended, purposes to be clarified, and values to be embraced. Being a Christian is definitely and certainly spiritual. But it is also physical. It involves muscle and bone, flesh and blood, land and sea, mountain and valley, village and town.

Good Christian teaching and preaching has insisted that the one be taken as seriously as the other. God created the heavens and the earth. Heavens, the realm of the spiritual, and earth, the realm of the physical. It is easy to find instances of people who take one and leave the other. We have specialists in things of the spirit who ignore things of the earth—people who are so heavenly minded that they do no earthly good. They are full of dreams and visions and pious sighs and beautiful thoughts, but somehow it never makes any difference in the way they treat their friends, conduct their business, or care about the world. And then there are people who are specialists in the material and ignore things of the spirit. They collect money, pursue sensations, play games, or accumulate possessions, but with all their devotion to the material, they never seem to become any better or happier or more useful. They are selfish and disgruntled and anxious.

So I want to talk about Jesus and geography. Jesus is the connection between the spiritual and the material. What God joins together, man puts asunder. But Jesus restores the break, healing the division between the seen and the unseen. The ministry of Jesus joins our lives to God's life, integrating earthly things to heavenly truths. He emphatically did not come to get our minds off the material so we could live like angels. And he did not come to get our minds off the spiritual so we could live like solid, no-nonsense citizens. His life put together what is split apart by our sin. He painstakingly integrates the two—God and geography.

The time we spent in Israel has been a stimulus to reflect on these things. Israel is a place associated preeminently with the life of the Spirit. But at the same time it is a very physical place. I want to use another physical place to understand some things about what it means to be a person who lives by faith in an invisible God on this visible earth.

Consider Nazareth. Three things are important about Nazareth: it was insignificant, advantageous, and dangerous.

Nazareth was insignificant. Nazareth is never mentioned in the Old Testament, never in the Talmud or Mishnah, never in Josephus's historical account written in the first century, and never in any other Greek or Roman writings. The town was totally insignificant. I have a friend who says he was born and raised in Butte, Nebraska, which isn't the end of the world, but on a clear day you can see it from there. That is Nazareth. The first mention of Nazareth in the Bible is by Luke: "The angel Gabriel was sent from God to a city of Galilee named Nazareth, to a virgin betrothed to a man whose name was Joseph . . . and the virgin's name was Mary" (Luke 1:26–27).

Today there is a magnificent church built over a cave where Mary might have been praying on that day. The Church of the Annunciation is visited by millions of people in the village where Mary was visited by the angel. That insignificant village is now a pilgrimage goal, a place where people go to remember that God has visited his people, and in response they worship and pray. The name Nazareth is now famous. In the Middle East, Christians are called in Hebrew and Arabic *Natsarim*—Nazareth people. But in Jesus's day that was not so. Nazareth was not included in anyone's travel plans. It was so obscure that it was something of a joke. When Nathanael was told about Jesus and that he came from Nazareth, he quipped, "Can anything good come out of Nazareth?" (John 1:46). Maybe God wanted to demonstrate to us that there is no place that is obscure to God. No piece of land, no village, no country, and no city that is unreachable, ignored, or forgotten. If it can happen in Nazareth, it can happen anywhere—and does.

Jesus spent his childhood, adolescence, and early adulthood in Nazareth. After that famous trip to Jerusalem with his parents when he was twelve years old, Jesus returned to Nazareth and "was obedient to them" and "increased in wisdom and in stature, and in favor with God and man" (Luke 2:51–52). Jesus lived in Nazareth for his first thirty years. All his development and education took place in this small village. He learned to walk and talk there. He played childhood games there. He developed a circle of friends there. He learned the trade of carpentry there.

Nazareth is advantageous. C. S. Lewis said that every seat in a theater has the best view of something.* And Nazareth, insignificant as it was, had the best view of something. And Jesus, it seems, took full advantage of what Nazareth offered.

---

* C. S. Lewis, *Christian Reflections* (Grand Rapids: Wm. B. Eerdmans, 1967), 10.

Nazareth

What was it like to grow up in Nazareth? Nazareth is nested in a basin of Galilean hills. There is a well at the center, the lowest part of the town. From there the hills rise on all sides steeply. There is no level ground in Nazareth. During our visit, we climbed up those hills to the rim of the basin and found a field of schoolchildren playing in recess from school. The crest of the hills is not far from anyplace in the village, and from the top—what a view spreads out before you! Great chunks of history are in panorama in the Esdraelon Valley with its twenty battlefields, which were the scenes of Barak's and Gideon's victories, Saul's and Josiah's defeats, and the struggles for freedom in the days of the Maccabees. There is Naboth's vineyard and the place of Jehu's revenge upon Jezebel; Shunem and the house of Elisha; Mount Carmel and the place of Elijah's sacrifice. To the east the valley of Jordan, with the range of Gilead; and to the west the radiance of the great Mediterranean Sea, with the ships of Spain and the promise of far explorations. You can see thirty miles in three directions. It is a map of Old Testament history.

But the view was more there than a picture book of the history of God's people. There was also action. Across the valley, opposite Nazareth, from the Samaritan hills emerged the road from

Jerusalem, thronged annually with pilgrims, and the road from Egypt with merchants going up and down. The Bedouin caravans could be watched for miles, coming up from the fords of Jordan, as well as the caravans from Damascus that wound around the foot of the hill on which Nazareth stands.

Nor can it have been only the eye that was stirred, for rumors and news from Rome entered Palestine close to Nazareth: information about the emperor's health, the changing influence of the statesmen, the Jew's prospects at Herod's court, Caesar's last order on the tax, and whether the policy of the procurator would be sustained. Some Galilean families must have had relatives in Rome. Jews would come back to this countryside to tell of life in the world's capital. Carried by peddlers, the scandals of Herod blazed up and down these roads, and the peripatetic rabbis would moralize upon them. The customs of the neighboring Gentiles—their loose living, their sensuous worship, their absorption in business, and the hopelessness of the inscriptions on their tombs, multitudes of which were readable (as some still are) on the roads around Galilee—would furnish endless talk in Nazareth.

Here Jesus grew up and suffered temptation. The perfection of his purity and patience was achieved not easily as behind a wide fence that shut the world out, but amid rumor and scandal. The pressure and problems of the world outside must have been acutely felt by the youth of Nazareth as by few others. Yet the scenes of Elijah's and Elisha's prophetic missions to it were also within sight.

A vision of the kingdoms of the world was possible from this village. In many ways, Nazareth was Jesus's Harvard and Yale.

Nazareth was dangerous. Shortly after Jesus began his public ministry, he was going through the towns of Galilee teaching in their synagogues. Luke reported that "he came to Nazareth, where he had been brought up; and he went to the synagogue, as his custom was, on the sabbath day" (Luke 4:16).

Jan and I visited what is probably that very synagogue. It was difficult for us to find in the winding, narrow streets just beyond the crowded bazaars. It is small, capable of seating at most thirty or forty people. Simple, spare, austere. Luke said,

> There was given to him the book of the prophet Isaiah. He
> opened the book and found the place where it was written,
> "The Spirit of the Lord is upon me,
> because he has anointed me to preach good news to
>   the poor.
> He has sent me to proclaim release to the captives
> and recovering of sight to the blind,
> to set at liberty those who are oppressed,
> to proclaim the acceptable year of the Lord." (verses 17–19)

And then, having read the scripture, he preached a one-line sermon: "Today this scripture has been fulfilled in your hearing" (verse 21). The response was immediate and positive. Those in the synagogue praised his gracious ways and clear speaking. Here was Joseph's son, whom they had known all their lives—they had watched him grow and develop, play in the streets, draw water from the well, climb the slopes, and gaze over the valley and roads. But Jesus didn't accept their response. He didn't want them to be impressed with his manner and his words but to open their lives to God. He saw through their praise. He saw that they were using compliments to mask their rejection of God. They were being nice to him so they would not have to take him seriously. At that moment, Jesus was in great danger—would he reduce himself to their expectations and fit into the old hometown ways? It would have been very easy to live out his life as the most popular man in town and be respected and revered.

But Jesus had not come back to his hometown to be admired. He wanted to bring the people to God. Jesus saw through their tactics and exposed them. He used the familiar names of Elijah and Elisha—both men had lived much of their lives in the valley stretched out below Nazareth—to challenge their small-minded comfortable selfishness that was glad to have Jesus entertain them with his sermon. When Jesus exposed their sentimentality and pretense, their nice compliments were replaced by murderous rage. They took him out of the synagogue and up a steep hill where there was a precipice. Their intent was to throw him off and kill him. He slipped through their midst and left. That is the last we hear of

Nazareth. It was Jesus's first rejection. And it was by the people with whom he had grown up.

Every village, town, and city has its distinctive ways of thinking and behaving. There are pressures to fit in. The pressures of Nazareth were on Jesus. But he didn't buckle. He loved Nazareth and had much to be grateful for in Nazareth, but he would not be reduced to Nazareth. Jesus could have lived out his life there as an admired person, but he wanted more for the people. He was in moral and spiritual danger of trading his ministry as the Christ for the indulgent respect of the townspeople. When he refused to do that, he was in danger of losing his life as they—insulted and reprimanded—tried to throw him off the cliff.

We all begin somewhere. Everyone has a hometown. The life of the gospel that Jesus demonstrated for us takes into account the details of that place, wherever it is. We often think that it would be easier to be a Christian if we lived somewhere else or if we went to another church, had better educational opportunities, or were better appreciated. In Nazareth, Jesus told us something quite different. Any place is the right place to be visited by God. Any place is full of advantages for growing "in stature, and in favor with God and man" (Luke 2:52). Any place is dangerous to the life of faith.

Amen.

Samaria

When it came close to the time for his Ascension, he gathered up his courage and steeled himself for the journey to Jerusalem. He sent messengers on ahead. They came to a Samaritan village to make arrangements for his hospitality. But when the Samaritans learned that his destination was Jerusalem, they refused hospitality. When the disciples James and John learned of it, they said, "Master, do you want us to call a bolt of lightning down out of the sky and incinerate them?"

Jesus turned on them: "Of course not!" And they traveled on to another village.

LUKE 9:51–56

In my school days, the dullest subject was geography. I don't know if that is a common feeling among schoolchildren, but for me, it was the bottom. Even the book was a disaster. Every geography book I can recall was oversized, so it was difficult to hold. The photographs were uninspired, the maps dull, and the statistical tables soporific. I hated it.

One year, when I was in fifth grade, I traveled by train with my mother into northern Saskatchewan in Canada. It was a long trip, nearly two thousand miles, and we were on the train for three days. It was my first long trip. I remember the endless fields and long stretches of empty land. The trees gradually diminished until our arrival at Prince Albert, where there was nothing to break the landscape except what the people there called bush-stunted, weatherbeaten trees, meager in both girth and stature. This was all new country to me, and I can still remember the stimulus and zest in smelling and experiencing a terrain and climate that was absolutely novel. Used to high, jutting peaks, I was now on a flatland that never stopped. Used to rich forests, I was now exposed to these sparse stands of trees. Used to towns of people, I was staying in a small farmhouse isolated on the empty northern prairie. The newness of it all and the great contrasts made a huge impression on me. What I didn't realize was that I was knee deep in geography.

When I returned home, I went to school, and among other things, I had a geography lesson. Before it had been the dullest hour of the day, but now, all of a sudden, I was transformed. My hand shot up at every opportunity. I wanted to tell the teacher and my classmates about the alkaline soil, the long ten-month Canadian winter, and the bush country. Geography was suddenly a subject full of shape and color. I had experienced it. It was no longer maps and charts and tables of figures. Now it was smells and feelings, remembered beauties and experienced difficulties.

Even today the word *geography* is a dull, flat word to me. Yet I have overcome my early prejudice against it, for the roads and mountains in the towns and cities of Palestine establish that Jesus is always involved in the here and now. Geography gives immediate texture to Jesus's acts and words. Jesus came to fulfill the prayer "On earth as it is in heaven" (Matthew 6:10). On earth—that is, geography.

One of the recurrent threats to a full life is abstraction—removing oneself from the specific and the concrete and existing in the general and the remote. Abstraction is letting a lot of opinions or systems or ideas or sentiments get between us and experienced reality. Grand ideas like "the love of God" get substituted by a clumsy hug or an awkward kiss. Ideal cities like Nazareth and Jerusalem get substituted by Bel Air and Baltimore.

In my own recent travel in Israel, I gathered fresh material to use in my personal and pastoral assault on the general and the abstract as I think of Jesus and read Scripture. Some of it I can use with you as we strive together to live immediately and attentively in the here and now of faith. Today's subject is Jesus in the countryside of Samaria.

Jesus walked a lot. It is obvious, but it is one of the obvious facts that I failed to realize the significance of until I did some walking in that country myself. One day we walked to Bethlehem. With a mile or so left to go and the sun getting hot, Jan had the temerity to wonder if walking made good sense when there were easily accessible buses and taxis. I reminded her that Joseph had not had to put up with that kind of second-guessing criticism from his wife as they walked that same road, and she had been nine months pregnant at the time. Read through the Gospels and note how often Jesus walked from Jerusalem to Nazareth, from Capernaum to Cana, to Nain, to Samaria, to Bethany, to the Jordan River, to Perea, to the wilderness, down to the sea, up to the mountain. Jesus walked a lot.

I have chosen Samaria as a place from which to reflect on Jesus walking through the country, for Samaria was a place that Jesus passed through as he went, each year, from Galilee to Jerusalem and back to Galilee. He never went around Samaria, but he went through it. Samaria is a kind of memorial of Jesus walking, of Jesus in transit.

For us, Samaria was a nice place to stop. It is halfway between Galilee and Jerusalem, and it is on a hill overlooking a fertile valley. We had a pleasant picnic on the mountain of Samaria on the day we were there, and we thought of Jesus making that trip each year along the road below us as his family and later his disciples made the Passover pilgrimage to Jerusalem.

And there is a lot to look at. The old city has excavations that show buildings from the time of Amos the prophet in the eighth century BC. There are impressive columns and other ruins from Roman times. A few miles down the road, there is a well by which Jesus sat and had that famous conversation with the Samaritan woman. As Jesus passed through Samaria and stopped and re-freshed himself, he met and talked with people who later were worked into his stories of the good Samaritan. In the gospel lesson for today, we read of Jesus's last trip through Samaria:

> When the days drew near for him to be received up, he set
> his face to go to Jerusalem. And he sent messengers ahead
> of him, who went and entered a village of the Samaritans,
> to make ready for him; but the people would not receive
> him, because his face was set toward Jerusalem. And when
> his disciples James and John saw it, they said, "Lord, do you
> want us to bid fire come down from heaven and consume
> them?" But he turned and rebuked them. And they went
> on to another village. (Luke 9:51–56)

Jesus's walk through Samaria was not just a Sunday break—he met hostility and difficulty there. We must not suppose that Jesus's walk was a pleasant afternoon stroll. Rather, it was the business of living that he was engaged in, in all its totality.

Day 16

Walking

At Samaria, at the end of a long day of walking, with more walking ahead the next day (the Jerusalem trip was about four days of walking, so this was midway), we realize how much experience Jesus had with the roads through the countryside and how extensively he used that experience in his teaching: the parable of the four kinds of soil, the parable of the mustard seed, the reference to lilies and thorns, the reference to the ravens and sparrows and fields white unto harvest, and the reference to vineyards and fig trees.

Jesus lived in close proximity to the soil of the land. He understood it and loved it. In today's language, we would say that he had a deep ecological awareness—everything was connected for Jesus. He taught in context. He was in touch with God (we take that for granted), and he was also in touch with creation (we sometimes forget that). Therefore he is in touch with all the reality that we are living in. Therefore what he teaches is true, and the way he guides us in pilgrimage is sound and practical. It works.

A few years ago a man told me a story of how he was developing some equipment for the army that was to be used in arctic conditions. He went for several weeks to Alaska to test it out to see if it actually worked in the conditions for which it was designed.

For the most part it was okay, but under actual field conditions, alterations had to be made. Modifications were introduced so that it was not only good in general but good specifically, in detail.

Jesus's life has that characteristic: it was field tested. He didn't work out his teaching in synagogue discussions with the rabbis. He didn't find himself a comfortable spot along the shore of the Sea of Galilee and offer his services as a consultant to the weary and confused in that province. And he didn't go to Jerusalem and establish his place among the religious authorities. He went to the country, walked along the roads, through the fields of wheat and the vineyards and the olive orchards. He went to where the people were— all kinds of people—in villages and cities, on main roads and back roads, climbing mountains and sailing on the sea. There was no place that Jesus did not go.

The walking is a fact, but it is also a metaphor. We become aware of this the moment we realize how frequently the metaphor is used in our biblical traditions. Jesus called himself "*the way*" (John 14:6). Jesus's disciples are repeatedly called *followers*. Paul instructed us how to "*walk* by the Spirit" (Galatians 5:16–26). The psalmist picked up the pace a little and said, "I will *run* in the way of thy commandments" (Psalm 119:32).

Luke emphasized this at the site of Samaria. After Jesus had been inhospitably turned away in Samaria, he continued on his way to Jerusalem:

As they were going along the road, a man said to him, "I will follow you wherever you go." And Jesus said to him, "Foxes have holes, and birds of the air have nests; but the Son of man has nowhere to lay his head." To another he said, "Follow me." But he said, "Lord, let me first go and bury my father." But he said to him, "Leave the dead to bury their own dead; but as for you, go and proclaim the kingdom of God." Another said, "I will follow you, Lord; but let me first say farewell to those at my home." Jesus said to him, "No one who puts his hand to the plow and looks back is fit for the kingdom of God." (Luke 9:57–62)

Each of these three men had ideas about following Jesus, and they had intentions to follow Jesus. But for some reason or another, they did not follow him. Ideas are very important in the life of faith. They are the mental tools by which we understand the total show and how we fit into it, but they are not enough. Good intentions are extremely important in the life of faith. They are the spark that gets things going, and without the spark there is no ignition. But good intentions are not enough. While sitting in an armchair, we can have any number of true ideas about God and ourselves and life, yet the ideas will never have any effect on our lives. We can come to church every Sunday of the year and be deeply moved by what is said and sung, and we can resolve to go out and do better next time but then promptly forget all about it. Jesus exposes the inadequacy of mere ideas and mere intentions in his challenge to the three people who said they would follow him. Because following Jesus is a physical act.

Following has become a masterful metaphor for the life of faith, for this means that we are faithfully putting into action what we learn with our minds and intend in our resolutions. We go someplace with Jesus. We travel. We walk.

Whatever else it is, walking is not just a means of getting somewhere. It is not only cheap transportation. It is a particular form of being in which body and mind and will are harmoniously joined. There is a sense of coordinated wholeness in walking. Henry David Thoreau, who was a great walker, wrote a wonderful essay on the meaning of walking, claiming not only physical benefits for it but also spiritual and moral benefits.* The virtual elimination of walking by the automobile has more than physical consequences, for it also diminishes spiritual perceptions. We get places faster, but we experience things less.

Following Jesus means that we are required to be completely there—all of us, not just our thoughts and our aspirations but also our muscles. Walking with Jesus means that great words like *faith, hope, love, repentance, forgiveness,* and *grace* are heard and experienced in the specific geographical conditions of our lives—these

---

* Henry David Thoreau, "Walking," *Atlantic,* June 1862, www.theatlantic.com/magazine /archive/1862/06/walking/304674/.

streets, office buildings, shopping malls, schools, and factories. Following Jesus doesn't mean making a beeline for heaven the fastest way we can. There is earth to be lived in and on.

One of the things that impressed us on our most recent trip to Israel was the schoolchildren on field trips. They were walking. Troops of children were walking from place to place with their teachers and often with armed soldiers for protection. One day we were watching these children tramp along near Caesarea on their way to examine a Roman aqueduct. We were talking to an Israeli who had emigrated from Yonkers, New York, to Israel in 1948—he was one of the original citizens of the new country. He told us that Israeli children are the "walkingest" children in the world. They walk the entire country. They learn to know the land on foot. They make the land their own by walking it. The hills and valleys, the markets and villages, the ruins and monuments all become stamped with their own personal experiences. That is very much the kind of thing that Jesus and his disciples were doing as they walked through the country and stopped to rest in Samaria. And it is what you and I are doing too: paying attention to the ground beneath us and the people around us, in company with Jesus so that what takes place in heaven also takes place on earth.

Amen.

Day 17

Exasperation

As they continued their travel, Jesus entered a village. A woman by the name of Martha welcomed him and made him feel quite at home. She had a sister, Mary, who sat before the Master, hanging on every word he said. But Martha was pulled away by all she had to do in the kitchen.

LUKE 10:38–40

This story of the two sisters, Mary and Martha, is a tough one for a pastor to deal with. It's next to impossible for a pastor to work up much enthusiasm for Mary as she is presented in this story that Luke tells us. But I'm going to try.

There is nothing more irritating than having a lot of work dumped on you, work that can't be put off, work that others are depending on you to do right now, and then have someone who knows what you are up against and is perfectly capable of helping instead sit around and do nothing. And if that person is your sister, brother, friend, or neighbor, that irritation quickly escalates into exasperation.

And it sure looks like that is what is happening in the Mary and Martha story. Jesus was traveling through a certain region and entered a village, and "a woman named Martha received him into her house" (Luke 10:38). We assume from other mentions of her name in the gospel accounts that they were longtime friends and that Martha's home was one in which Jesus felt at home. Martha was a generous person. She was hospitable, and her house had open doors. But Jesus's passing through the village was also unscheduled, so she had no idea he was going to show up just then. Martha loved Jesus, but he also had the annoying habit of showing up unannounced and always at mealtimes. Why couldn't he send a message—what are angels for, anyway? She was caught unprepared and not for the first time. She went to work in a frenzy. There was a bed to make up and meals to plan. She had just finished washing the bedsheets from the guests who had left yesterday, and they were drying out on the clothesline in the courtyard. She was out of olive oil and cucumbers and had to run to the market to get the makings for a salad.

Meanwhile some of the neighbors had heard that Jesus had arrived unexpectedly and several of them came over to greet him and listen to him talk—everyone always loved listening to Jesus tell stories and talk about the kingdom. His speech was so colorful, and he was so wise. You could ask him anything, and when he started talking it wasn't like anything you had ever heard. Every sentence was so fresh and sharply phrased. So it wasn't surprising that the neighbors were there, sitting around on the floor, listening to Jesus. And Martha loved to have it so—she loved having people in her home and loved having Jesus there as her guest. Yes, there was a lot to do, but Martha really didn't mind.

But that day she was a bit overwhelmed. Just then she came running in from the market with a bag of grapes in one hand and a cup of flour that she had borrowed from a neighbor in the other. She was going to make some pita bread to go with the salad. And there, right before her, was her sister, Mary, sitting on the floor with the neighbors, listening to Jesus teach.

That was the last straw. What's with Mary, anyway? Martha was understandably upset. She snapped at Jesus: "Lord, do you not care that my sister has left me to serve alone? Tell her then to help me" (Luke 10:40).

And do you know what? Jesus wouldn't do it. Not only did he refuse to get Martha some help, he turned on her—criticized her, of all things! He said, "Martha, Martha, you are anxious and troubled about many things" (verse 41). We don't have Martha's response, but any one of us can supply it: "You bet I'm anxious and troubled about many things. What do you expect? Here you drop in on us without any warning and right at mealtime. The house is a mess; there's no food on hand—do you have any idea of all the stuff I have to do? And my sister, my precious little sister, the 'spiritual' one, leaves it all to me. And you don't even care!"

But Jesus hadn't finished. While Martha was still fuming, muttering under her breath and stomping off into the kitchen, she heard Jesus not only refusing to rebuke Mary's irresponsible spirituality but commending Mary as if she were doing something wonderful. He said, "Mary has chosen the good portion, which shall not be taken away from her" (verse 42).

Well, there you have it. I have just imagined the circumstances of this story of Martha, Mary, and Jesus the way I most often have heard it referred to: Jesus is great at the business of salvation, but he doesn't quite get it when it comes to running a household or a business. And it's wonderful that some people get to sit around and listen to Jesus teach, but those same people would go hungry much of the time if it wasn't for the rest of us who know how to pitch in and get things done. But let's keep following the story.

Day 18

Details

I have reconstructed the story in the terms most of us commonly hear it. But I left out some details that change things considerably. A closer look will convince you, I think, that Luke didn't include this story to engage our sympathies with Martha and our impatience with Mary and Jesus.

The first detail is this. There is nothing Jesus was more insistent upon than that we, his followers, serve one another: "Whoever would be great among you must be your servant, and whoever would be first among you must be slave of all. For the Son of man also came not to be served but to serve, and to give his life as a ransom for many" (Mark 10:43–45) and "Which is the greater, one who sits at the table, or one who serves? Is it not the one who sits at the table? But I am among you as one who serves" (Luke 22:27). The servant life is the Christian life. And servant living involves a lot of behind-the-scenes drudge work with unexpected assignments. No, whatever Martha was being reprimanded for, it was not her hospitality or her servant life in that household.

But pay attention to the first sentence in this passage: "As they went on their way, [Jesus] entered a village" (10:38). We just happen to know where Jesus was going when he stopped in this village—he was going to Jerusalem. A couple of pages earlier we are told, "When the days drew near for him to be received up, he set his face to go to Jerusalem" (9:51). That's a signal that we are getting close to the conclusion of this story—no more digressions, no more asides, for we're headed for the end. For the next ten chapters, Luke told us what happened on this final trip to Jerusalem. Basically Jesus was conducting a traveling seminar on how to live the Christian life after he leaves. He was going to die in Jerusalem. After his resurrection and ascension, these followers were going to continue his kingdom work. He was training them to continue. In other words, Jesus was carefully and in detail preparing people like us for the kind of speaking and acting that are appropriate for our daily lives when he'll be with us through the Holy Spirit but no longer physically present.

We know that the training seminar was coming to a conclusion when Luke says in chapter 19 that Jesus "was was near to Jerusalem" and then that "he went on ahead, going up to Jerusalem" (verses 11, 28). The next event is the Palm Sunday entrance, which sets off the events of Holy Week: the Passion, Crucifixion, and Resurrection. When we read a paragraph in the gospel, we can't understand it if we remove it from the story as a whole. And the story as a whole is absolutely critical here. When we recognize this context—this intense teaching and training period just before the Jerusalem climax—we will look at this story a little differently and notice a word that I passed over earlier: *distracted*.

Luke tells us, "Martha was distracted with much serving," and

Jesus addressed Martha, saying: "You are anxious and troubled about many things" (10:40–41). Distracted is not quite the same thing as being practical, working hard, and taking the tasks of hospitality seriously. Distracted means "not paying attention." It means not having a center or an anchor, being pulled this way and that by whoever and whatever. Luke set Jesus's presence in the home of Martha and Mary that day at a time when Jesus was pulling everything together and gathering everyone who was willing into the holy community that would continue to give witness and live in obedience to him.

Jesus was the center. As the days were drawing to a conclusion, every word was important. There was going to be a lot to do— healing and teaching, preaching and hospitality, suffering and helping— and they needed to learn to do it the way Jesus did it. They had just been told, "The harvest is plentiful, but the laborers are few; pray therefore the Lord of the harvest to send out laborers into his harvest" (verse 2). If they didn't learn to speak Jesus's words and do his work in his way, they would either quickly burn out or end up using his reputation as a front for their own selfish ambition. When we look at it that way, it turns out that Mary was the practical one and Martha the impractical one. Mary was listening to Jesus. She was listening so she would know what to do and how to do it. By listening, her imagination was being shaped in how to recognize the needs of her neighbor. She was learning how to discern between showy religion and down-to-earth love. She was realizing how prayer is personal and immediate and how it is different from manipulation and magic. She was realizing how destructive it is to treat people as objects and functions and how freeing it is to receive everything and everyone as a gift. And much, much more.

And Martha was not listening—not listening to Jesus, who was there to train and prepare her to live for the glory of God in the days just ahead when he would no longer be dropping in for a bed and a meal. Men and women who don't listen usually do too much and do much of it the wrong way.

A few years ago we were having our home south of Lakeside remodeled. My dad had built the original structure fifty-three years ago, and we were now getting it ready to live in ourselves. We were living in Vancouver while much of the work was done, but our daughter, Karen, was there one day when the workmen were tearing out an interior wall. At one point a worker exclaimed, "Wow! I've never seen so many nails in one wall in all my life. I wonder who put this up!" Karen said, "My grandpa did that—he wanted to make sure it would stay." My dad was a pretty good builder, but he didn't always know what he was doing. And when he was in doubt, he used more nails.

When Karen told me that story, I remembered how Roger Bannister, the man who first ran the four-minute mile, described his venture into carpentry. He said he made up for his lack of skill by using a lot of nails.

There is nothing we need more teaching and training in than simply living—living to the glory of God, living for Jesus, living in love and faith and hope, living in patience and gentleness, living sacrificially and hospitably, living with our children and our parents, living with dignity and in joy. And there is no one more accessible and present and skilled at teaching us than Jesus. That's why we keep coming back to this sanctuary Sunday after Sunday, to sit at Jesus's feet and listen to his Word. We're learning how to live all the details of our lives in the company of Jesus.

Amen.

Prudent

All this time his older son was out in the field. When the day's work was done he came in. As he approached the house, he heard the music and dancing. Calling over one of the houseboys, he asked what was going on. He told him, "Your brother came home. Your father has ordered a feast—barbecued beef!—because he has him home safe and sound."

The older brother stalked off in an angry sulk and refused to join in.

Luke 15:25–28

The parable of the prodigal exposes our inner lives. If we look attentively we will see ourselves in it, and we will see God. This is our biography and God's grace. There are numerous opportunities to see what we look like in the Scriptures, but none that have cut through the pretensions of the human heart as effectively as this parable. We look in a mirror to see what we look like physically and outwardly. We can go to a psychiatrist to see what we look like emotionally and inwardly. But we go to the Bible to see what we look like in relationship with God. In the mirror of Scripture, we are faced with the man created by God, alienated from God, and sought out by God.

This is a story of two sons and their father. Much has been made of the first son (the so-called prodigal) and his father (the God who waited for him). But today let us look at the older son, the son who might be called prudent. Both sons need to be considered, and too often this second son is ignored. Together they function like those multiple mirrors in clothing stores. Looking straight ahead, you think everything looks okay—then suddenly in the second mirror, you see a side view or a back view and things look worse. Perhaps we looked at the prodigal son and immediately referred him to someone else. But if we keep looking at the parable, maybe we will suddenly see ourselves reflected in the older son.

One scholar described these sons as "the one who strayed and the one who stayed."* What was this second son, this one who stayed, like? As we ask the question, we remember that we are really asking, "What are we like?"

The household in the parable consisted of a father and two sons. Restless under the restrictions at home, the younger son asked for his part of the inheritance and received it and then jauntily set off to see the world and have a little fun. It was a foolish thing to do, and it turned out badly. He lived high, but he was soon brought low. The zest and excitement ended in a famine, and he was reduced to feeding pigs—the lowest job a Jew could hold.

Nothing is said about the elder brother through this time. But it is not difficult to reconstruct his feelings from his later reactions. Our first impulse would be to admire the elder brother—after all, he had put aside any irrational desires, worked hard, and stayed with his father, giving himself responsibly to the life before him. He took life seriously and did a good job. From the outside his life might appear colorless, but at least it was worthwhile.

But all the time, he was seething inside. His brother was out having all the fun, and he was left with all the responsibilities. His

---

* Donald G. Miller, *The Gospel According to Luke,* The Layman's Bible Commentary 18 (Louisville, KY: John Knox, 1959), 120.

brother was squandering the family estate, and he was day by day trying to keep it together. He became "the center of his life circle, and the center grew so black that soon the whole circle was black. His was pride of temperament, which is perhaps harder to cure than pride of flesh, as a virus in the blood is harder to cure than a gaping wound."*

When the younger son was welcomed home after his years of spendthrift living, the older brother's brooding erupted like an angry volcano. He sullenly refused to participate in the homecoming. And what he said shows what he had been feeling the entire time.

> He was jealous of the gaiety of his younger brother, and
> doubly jealous when the prodigal was welcomed with
> feasting. He was as self-righteous as he was jealous,
> pointing out that the younger son: "devoured thy living
> with harlots" is an unsparing condemnation. He was as
> self-pitying as he was jealous and self-righteous: "these
> many years and thou never gavest me a kid" are of the
> essence of self-pity. Jealousy, self-righteousness, and
> self-pity all come from an inward turning eye: the elder
> brother, while pretending to worship God, was his own

---

* George Arthur Buttrick, ed., *The Interpreter's Bible: Luke, John* 8 (Nashville: Abingdon, 1982), 271.

god. . . . While the younger son was prodigal in body, at least part of his heart was at home; but the elder brother was prodigal at heart, and only his body was at home.*

There is little that is attractive in the elder brother, the prudent son who calculated his own changes and avoided any reckless dissipation of his chances in the world.

---

* Buttrick, *The Interpreter's Bible*, 279.

Day 20

Ourselves

How did the second son get that way? Remember though, we are talking about ourselves. He began with a wrong attitude toward his father. He treated his father as an employer. He had his routine, and he knew what the commandments were and kept them. He knew his father was the boss, and he served him. He served and obeyed his father, but there is no evidence that he was a son to the father. He didn't spend the kind of time with his father that could lead to the enjoyment of one person with another. He had his own life to live, and he was living it on his own. He did his duty and kept the rest to himself.

When the life of the church becomes a list of rules to be kept and a service to be rendered, it has become stuffy and unbearable beyond description. There are rules to be kept and services to be rendered—our Lord has commanded many things—but they are not the life of our faith; the Father is. If by doing his work we neglect him, things are thrown out of balance and the distortion becomes so hideous that even preachers can talk about attractive sinners and stale saints. "What a wretched thing it is to call oneself a Christian and yet be a stranger and a grumbling servant in the Father's house."*

* Helmut Thielicke, *The Waiting Father: Sermons on the Parables of Jesus,* trans. John W. Doberstein (Cambridge, England: Lutterworth, 1959), 40.

This wrong attitude toward his father developed into a wrong attitude toward his brother. The prudent son had a very low regard for his prodigal brother. He judged him mercilessly. He said, "This son of yours . . . has devoured your living with harlots" (Luke 15:30). Nothing more scathing could have been said. He saw his brother as a worn-out sinner, not as a returned brother. He looked on him as the one who had broken the rules and when it was no longer fun had come home. The fact that he once had enjoyed his younger brother's company in the house and would enjoy it once again counted for nothing. He looked on the outside world through legal spectacles. He noticed sins, not his brother. He saw a pattern of morality, not a person. He was substituting a lifeless and gloomy set of morals for the exciting and joyous world of personal relationships.

Because of his harsh judgment, he alienated himself from his brother. There is a very significant change of pronouns. He said, "This son of yours" (verse 30), not "this brother of mine." He would not associate with anyone who had behaved so badly. He would not be tainted by any kinship with a prodigal. The prodigal was his father's son but not his brother's brother. But when he denied brotherhood, he also forfeited sonship. The feast that his father was giving was a feast for the whole household. The prudent son, in his anger, refused to take part.

The primary thrust of the story is not on the prodigal or the prudent but on the father. The father's acceptance of the prodigal—

the acceptance that so infuriated the elder brother—was based on grace. The elder brother, not understanding this, would not participate in it. But even with this son's self-righteous anger, the father would not thereby leave him alone. He went out and entreated him to come in, assuring him that he had access to everything too. "Son, you are always with me, and all that is mine is yours" (verse 31). He was a father to both the prodigal and the prudent. He would not slight either at the expense of the other.

This acceptance and restoration are a picture of God's grace, which gives before it commands and loves before it is loved. The elder son could not understand the father's joy, which was the result not of the younger brother's behavior but of the fact that he had once more taken shelter in his love and had become a son. The father still loved the elder brother, but he could not refuse sonship to the prodigal because of his brother's objections. God's acceptance of a man is for God's own reasons, and he will not be dictated to by our own ideas of who is fit for the fellowship of his house.

Some of us will see ourselves in the reflection of the prodigal son, and others in the prudent son. For some there has been a trip into the far country. For others life has been more conventional. Most of us will catch glimpses of ourselves in the double mirror provided by both the sons. Both prodigality and prudence separate us from God. They are very nearly the same thing in the eyes of God, for they remove us from the fellowship of the Father, whose desire is that we should live openly and happily in his will.

Prodigality removes us from the Father by outward rebellion. Prudence removes us by inward separation. We look at the two brothers from the outside and see good guys and bad guys. God looks at them from the inside and sees two sons who have both severed their relationship with their father. And not only do prodigality and prudence both separate us from God, but they also put massive barriers between brothers. The prodigal despises the prudent, and the prudent has contempt for the prodigal. The careful man has nothing to do with the reckless big spender, who in turn thinks it is a dull business to be around his pious brother. And so we cut ourselves out from the fellowship with the Father.

The father has the last word of the parable as he rejoices in finding the one who was lost and urges the prudent brother to join in. "It was fitting to make merry and be glad, for this your brother was dead, and is alive; he was lost, and is found" (verse 32). Similarly, the church might be called the Society of Those Who Rejoice with God.

Amen.

John

So Loved

This is how much God loved the world: He gave his Son, his one and only Son. And this is why: so that no one need be destroyed; by believing in him, anyone can have a whole and lasting life. God didn't go to all the trouble of sending his Son merely to point an accusing finger, telling the world how bad it was. He came to help, to put the world right again.

JOHN 3:16–17

A good friend recently made an observation that has intrigued me. He said a lot of Christians have two basic reactions to the world: they are angry at it, or they are afraid of it. I had never thought of it just that way before, but since hearing him say it and then being observant of what was going on around me, I think he is right. For the past couple of weeks, I've been collecting data to test out his assertion—fragments of conversations from the people with whom I live and work, observations of their responses and reactions. Most of the items fall into one of two categories: fear or anger, which interchange at times of trouble and crisis. And do you know something else? In looking at the actual life situations of those who are angry or fearful, I don't blame them. In fact, I am one of them. There is a lot to be afraid of in this world. As there is also a lot to be angry at.

In the course of thinking about my friend's statement and testing it out with my own experiences, I came to this text in John's gospel: "For God so loved the world that he gave his only Son, that whoever believes in him should not perish but have eternal life. For God sent the Son into the world, not to condemn the world, but that the world might be saved through him" (3:16–17).

Three things jumped out of that text in a fresh way to me. First, the love God has for the world is the great fact we have to deal with. It is the fact that defines the world. God loves the world. What a contrast to what I do. I am alternately fearful of the world, and then I am angry with it. God steadily loves the world. It seems to me that God has even more cause to be angry with the world than I have. He created a world of beauty and wholeness. He designed a creation stunning in complexity and intricacy. He established purposes filled with meaning and pleasure. And man and woman were the crown of his creation, marvelous beings capable of understanding its brilliance, feeling its beauty, and participating in its purposes. And what happened? They thoroughly messed it up. And we thoroughly mess it up. If I were God, I would be angry and have everyone stand to account.

It also seems to me that God has even more cause to be fearful of the world than I have. Billions of these people who have been created by God for love have instead used their creative will rebelliously and defiantly. The history books tell the story of the evil choices that have been made, and the newspapers tell the continuation of those choices. The accumulated results of these evil choices are evident all around us—violence and disorder, malice and greed, hate and cruelty, boredom and selfishness. And things are getting worse, it seems, instead of better. Is the world now, after all these centuries, unmanageable and unredeemable? If I were God, I would escape to some far-off corner of the universe while old planet Earth ate itself to death.

From what I can see, God should be good and angry, and good and scared. But he is neither. God so loves the world. The prevalence of evil doesn't throw him into a paroxysm of anger but into an act of love. The power of evil doesn't send him reeling into a fearful retreat but into an aggressive encounter in which love wins. God loves the world. Our reactions to the world are no help in understanding God's responses. His response, though, is the greatest help in changing ours.

Day 22

Eternal Life

T he second thing that John's text showed me is that the love God has for the world has enormous consequences in the lives we live every day. And the consequences are all happy: "not perish . . . have eternal life . . . not to condemn . . . saved" (John 3:16–17). The practical result of God's love for the world is that we get what he has. We share the life of God himself. His love works, and it makes something happen. It is creative. It is redemptive. It changes things—anger into joy, fear into peace. Jesus's comprehensive phrase is "eternal life."

Eternal. It means that which comes from God. It is not a word that refers to the future. Eternal life is not the life we get after we die. It is the life we get from God right now. I got a biological life from my parents, but I get eternal life from the Spirit of God. It is not something I wait for but something I participate in. It is not a distant promise but a present history.

Life. It is an ordinary word that John packed with extraordinary meaning. Life, for many of us, is reduced to just getting by. It is bored, routine, humdrum. Thoreau wrote of those who live "lives of quiet desperation."* But that is not God's will. That is not

---

* Henry David Thoreau, *Walden: Or, Life in the Woods* (New York: Houghton Mifflin, 1910), 8.

life under his love. Rather, life is resonant with a wide range of joy and meaning, complex with strands of purpose and peace, and vibrant with the profundities of righteousness and love. A person is never wholly and fully alive until he or she is alive to God. By being alive to God, we are capable of responding and participating on every level of existence, from the lowest to the highest and back again. As we become alive to God, we don't become less human and more angelic but just the opposite. All our inherent energies and abilities are developed and matured to peaks of intensity.

In a world defined by anger, our lives are narrowed into bitterness and violence. In a world defined by fear, our lives become anemic and timid. In a world defined by God's love, the result is eternal life.

Christians

The third insight released by John 3:16–17 in a fresh way for me is this: the love God has for the world is put into action by what he did in Christ, and it is an action in which we participate. I never kept a record, and my memory is somewhat faulty by this time, but I think I have fallen in love publicly thirty to forty times. The earliest time of which I have a clear recollection was in the first grade. These earthquakes continued at a rate of one or two a year. One of the significant things about these love affairs was that the girl, in the majority of the instances, never knew about it. I wanted her to know, but I didn't know how to say it. I wanted to express my romance, but I was fearful of rejection or scorn. And so I languished in a swamp of sentiment. And nothing ever came of it. My love never made anything happen.

You can't say that about God's love. His love does make something happen. The commonest misunderstanding that we have of love is that it is a feeling, a sentiment, a flutter in our stomachs, a tremor in our knees. But the love God has for the world is not a sugary sentiment. It is an effective action: God gave his only Son. And that action makes a connection between his love and our lives, between what he wants for us and what we need from him.

Jesus Christ is the action—a life lived in sacrifice and suffering, in truth and obedience, and in crucifixion and resurrection. God so loved the world that we might have eternal life. God's love and our eternal lives are connected by the Son. His love is made effective in our lives, not in the announcement sent out that he loves us but by the action of giving Jesus. Christ is born into our lives. This action makes God's love effective in us. It faces the evil and hostility of men, and by conquering that, it brings about our salvation.

A number of years ago a very important book was written by the Old Testament scholar George Ernest Wright, with the title *God Who Acts*. Professor Wright focused attention on a perfectly obvious but frequently overlooked feature of the biblical story: we know God from his actions. We have no Word of God that is "just" a word. We do not have distilled divine teachings in the Scriptures. We have a story of what God has done: sending and giving his son for our salvation. There are words, to be sure, but the words always are either introducing or interpreting an event that is an action of God.

John's gospel begins, "In the beginning was the Word," and then quickly follows with "And the Word became flesh and dwelt among us, full of grace and truth; we have beheld his glory" (verses 1, 14). In this action, God invited our participation. Belief is the response we make to accept and participate in what God did in love for us in Christ. Belief is sharing in obedience and praise the life of Christ present among us.

I need to admit to you that I still get angry with the world and still become fearful in it. I get fits of righteous indignation in which I judge and condemn. I descend into moods of fear when all I want to do is escape. But I have learned not to make a religion out of my anger or my fear. For I have become convinced that God is not angry and God is not fearful. Insofar as I continue to be angry and fearful, it is only a sign of my immaturity and my sin. But I am learning to serve the Lord who loves the world and who puts that love into an action in which I can participate. I'm learning to receive that love in a present eternal life.

And I know a lot of other people who are learning to do the same thing. We are called Christians.

Amen.

Day 24

Before

"Believe me," said Jesus, "*I am who I am* long before Abraham was anything."

That did it—pushed them over the edge. They picked up rocks to throw at him. But Jesus slipped away, getting out of the Temple.

JOHN 8:58–59

This gospel lesson opens with a raging argument. Jesus and the Jews were arguing with each other. They were calling each other names. Then it became hostile. Jesus told the Jews that they were sons of the devil. They returned the charge, adding a slur on his family origins by calling him a Samaritan. Jesus called them bastards. They called him demon possessed. Jesus called them liars. They called him a blasphemer.

It is hard to get at the root of the controversy. But fix it in your mind that there was a controversy. Something happened between Jesus and these religious persons in the temple that caused the blood pressure of both parties to rise. Something deep within both was touched by the words and responses. There was nothing cool or deliberate about the meeting. Manners were left in the outer court. A careful reader of Scripture knows that there is something inevitable about this hostile confrontation. Something like this had to come about sooner or later. And we will never understand the significance of Jesus Christ if we do not understand the rage he can provoke.

I wonder, have you ever felt really angry at God? It would be surprising if you had not. If there is any seriousness to the love you have for him, there is also likely to have been anger and hate at

some point. The reason is that a meeting with Christ involves ulti-
mates. He faces us with a radical decision. His presence no longer
permits nondecision, noncommitment, nonparticipation, or neu-
trality. But there is a part of our personalities that would rather
drift. There is a tendency in every man to avoid the real and the
ultimate. But it is a tendency that our Lord has no intention of al-
lowing to go on unchecked, for this tendency is a sickness (a sin). It
debilitates our lives. It ruins our eternal constitutions. It is not our
nature, but it is our fallen nature, and if we are to have any health,
joy, and fullness, we must deal with it.

Christ has an unrelieved, persistent challenge for us to face
God in our common existence, and that is what is at the base of any
anger we might feel toward Christ—his unrelieved, persistent challenge to face God in our common existence. Our inability to avoid
this demand sometimes sparks hostility.

Characteristically, when we examine an event in the life of
Jesus Christ, we find a probing revelation of something in us and
an illuminating revelation of something in God. The probing revelation of ourselves that we find here is that whenever we oppose
God, it is for moral, not rational or intellectual, reasons. Jesus said
to the Jews, "Which of you convicts me of sin? If I tell the truth,
why do you not believe me? He who is of God hears the words of
God; the reason why you do not hear them is that you are not of
God" (John 8:46–47).

We give the strangest reasons for not being serious servants of

God. We spin the most elaborate arguments to defend our disobedient lives. We weave a fabric of rationalizations that give some surface respectability to lives lived far from the center of God's redemptive action in Jesus Christ. Harry Stack Sullivan once said that rationalization is "giving a plausible and often exceedingly inconsequential explanation."*

Jesus spoke God's Word to men. They gave plausible but exceedingly inconsequential explanations for refusing him. One thing they said was that their father was Abraham, which meant, I guess, that they had a pretty good family background. Apparently they intended it as a defense against obeying Jesus—which had plausibility. But it was inconsequential because nothing Jesus said contradicted Abraham. All he did was bring God's covenant with Abraham to a personal, contemporary completeness—and to a point of decision.

They said Jesus had a demon. That was plausible; he certainly had a special kind of energy, an uncommon relationship with the supernatural, and he was a disruptive force in many of the traditional institutions of the day. But it was inconsequential since what was being asked for was not their theological evaluation but their moral obedience. The discussion about demons was what we today call "the red herring"—a diversionary tactic that takes one's attention from the central action. In athletics, it's called "the fake."

---

* Henry Stack Sullivan, *The Interpersonal Theory of Psychiatry* (London: Routledge, 2001), 113.

Jesus struck back with impatience at their combination of plausibility and inconsequentiality. "Which of you convicts me of sin?" (verse 46). He sliced through the jungle growth of their excuse making and fault finding. "Where is the evil in what I am doing? If you want to talk, let us talk about basics: 'Who convicts me of sin?'" That is the question. If you can't discredit Jesus Christ on ultimate grounds, then you must listen to him. He won't let you make conversation around the periphery.

I AM

The Jews wanted to talk about Jesus, but he wanted them to decide about him. They wanted to get into an argument, but he wanted to get into a relationship with them.

We very often make a great play at getting all the facts before committing ourselves. In a kind of pseudoscientific ritual, we consider and study and discuss but never put the pieces together and become that which we are being called to be. "Objectivity is the rationalization for moral disengagement, the classic cop-out from choice-making."*

Some people reject God because they don't like what certain denominations are doing in the field of race relations. Some will not worship God because they prefer other pastoral leadership. Some refuse to make any financial commitment to the needs of the world because they do not believe the scripture that says it is Christ who is hungry and ill-clothed in the poverty and need of mankind. Christ's words come ever more insistently: "Which of you convicts me of sin? If I tell the truth, why do you not believe me?" (John 8:46).

The reason you are not obeying God is not because of the

---

* Andrew Kopkind

Presbyterians or the pastors or the administrators or other Christians or non-Christians. It is because you hate God. But you really do not have the honesty to say that, so you give some exceedingly plausible but highly inconsequential explanation. That is what Jesus was saying. It's a small wonder that some people became angry. Caught in such an exposure, I get a little angry myself.

The illuminating revelation of God that we find here is that there is nothing useful or of value in our lives for which Christ is not the previous beginning point and the present fulfillment. It is summarized at the conclusion of this gospel lesson as Jesus made the resounding affirmation: "Before Abraham was, I am" (verse 58). In this discussion, Abraham had become a symbolic figure. He more or less stood for things as they were, as they had come from the past to the present, with religious action and historical legitimacy. The Jews were sons of Abraham, which is to say that they were pretty much okay the way they were. They had a good background and a distinguished past.

Abraham then became an excuse for refusing God's Word in Christ. Since things were not disastrous, there was no need for the miraculous. Since they had good lives at the present, there was no need for doing anything radical to them. Abraham became an attempt at self-justification. He was the memory of two thousand years of survival. He was the reassurance of their identity. He was the source of pride and aspiration. Since they were sons of Abraham, nothing could be completely off base. Jesus didn't deny Abraham's

great significance. He never comes to our lives to destroy, elimi-
nate, or devastate. He didn't say that we are all wrong and that we
have to give up everything in order to be right. He didn't say that
we are nothing. He wasn't contemptuous of Abraham.

He said, "Before Abraham was, I am." In other words, he is
previous to everything that Abraham was and is to them. Christ is
the priority. Jesus is before any of that which they value so highly.
Jesus is not a latecomer who is adding his two cents to everything
that has already been said through the years by Abraham, Moses,
David, Socrates, Confucius, and Buddha. He is previous to all of it,
preexistent. He is the first cause, the primary source. He is that
which is eternally at the beginning. That means that when God
appears to us he is not something or someone to be added on or not
added on to everything else that we have experienced, thought, and
supposed. He antedates everything. He is not an option to a style
of life about which we can make a peripheral choice. He is the beginning of life itself.

That doesn't destroy Abraham or anything else that might
have value in our lives. But it does cast it into a new mode of existence. By being before, Jesus becomes the meaning and eternal
presence of God in everything that has come previously. We cannot take our past and have it mean anything without also taking
him. We cannot prefer our present to him because he is already in
our present. We cannot opt for any alternatives that have come
down to us through the years, because before they were, he is.

Do you see what that does to our rationalizations, our intellectualizations, our avoidances, and our failure to decide? It exposes them, yes. But it also redeems them. The question is not whether the Jews choose between Abraham and Jesus. The question is whether they will live obediently to God now.

Who is your Abraham? Who or what do you use as the legitimizing presence for your current disobedience? Your family, your profession, your work, your house, your religion, your moral or physical issues, your childhood, your disappointments, your successes, your failures?

Christ doesn't disdain anything you say. He has no contempt for anything in your life. But he does say, "Before that was, I am."

Amen.

Day 26

Misunderstanding

The crowd that had been with him when he called
Lazarus from the tomb, raising him from the dead,
was there giving eyewitness accounts. It was because
they had spread the word of this latest God-sign that
the crowd swelled to a welcoming parade. The Phari-
sees took one look and threw up their hands: "It's out
of control. The world's in a stampede after him."

JOHN 12:17–19

J ohn set three things together for this message: the anointing of Jesus, the plot to kill Jesus, and the parade to praise Jesus. Together, the three events show how God used what look like disparate and contradictory things to form a unity to develop our salvation. We work differently; we sort things out into good and bad, useful and useless, strong and weak, proper and improper. We affirm one grouping and discard the other. We try to capture what will help us and get rid of what will harm us. But God doesn't throw anything away. He takes whatever occurs—whatever we offer him—and fashions a salvation out of it.

Look at what is presented to him here: a woman's extravagance, the malice of a group of conspirators, and the cheerful but obviously shallow enthusiasm of a great crowd. Each of the incidents is the result of misunderstanding Jesus, and any one by itself would seem to be poor material to launch the series of events we know as Jesus's Passion, which climaxes in the Crucifixion and Resurrection. Combining them would seem to simply compound the misunderstanding.

The theme of misunderstanding is a submotif in John's gospel. He gave several instances in which Jesus did or said something and the hearer (or observer) wildly misunderstood. But the story doesn't break off at that point. By showing how Jesus used the very act of misunderstanding, John wanted to develop belief. For instance, Jesus said to Nicodemus, "You must be born anew" (John 3:7). Nicodemus heard a promise of renewed youth, a dream that has deceived many both before and since. But Jesus was talking about a spiritual birth that brings us into eternal life, and he continued the conversation until Nicodemus responded in faith. Another instance of misunderstanding is Jesus's conversation with the Samaritan woman at the well. Jesus said, "Whoever drinks of the water that I shall give him will never thirst" (4:14). The woman, tired of drawing water from a well on a hot day, thought he was offering to relieve her of that round of fatiguing work. She misunderstood. But Jesus continued the conversation until she responded to the offer of eternal life.

In each case, when misunderstanding occured, John showed how it was used by Jesus in such a way that his truth was finally realized and received. The misunderstanding became a means toward comprehension. It became a way to truth.

We are, it seems, so filled with questions, so racked with needs, so clamorous with desires, that when anything approximating an answer, a fulfillment, or a completion appears, we immediately try to fit it to our demands. And in our greediness and our haste, we almost inevitably misunderstand. We don't have the education, the experience, or the ability to comprehend what God says to us. Our first understandings of the truth of Christ are always misunderstandings. But the consequence is not to flunk out. We are not rejected as candidates for the gospel. Rather, he continues the conversation and after each give-and-take of question and answer and acceptance and doubt, we gain a closer approximation of the truth. Jesus uses our ignorance, our prejudices, and our needs as means for us to gain comprehension of his truth and our salvation.

To see how this works, imagine yourself driving along the highway by yourself and seeing a large sign alongside the road, Love Your Neighbor, and right beneath it, Gasoline: 50 Cents a Gallon. You notice that your tank is nearly empty, and you are impressed by the piety of the owner, so you turn in. An attendant comes to you, and you say, "Fill 'er up." He leaves, but instead of going to the gasoline pump, he goes to a shelter where there are several people seated, and he brings them back to your car, opens your doors, and installs them in the seats. He then comes around to you and says, "Thank you for responding to our invitation to love your neighbor. All of these people in your car need a ride. I appreciate you taking your Christian faith seriously enough to express it in a practical way." You are bewildered and a little angry. You say, "When I said, 'Fill 'er up,' I meant the gasoline tank, not the car." The attendant replies, "Oh, you must have misunderstood our sign."

That little fantasy has all the ingredients of what happens not only quite often in the church with the gospel but also in nearly every detail of daily life. We have certain expectations of what we want other people to do for us, and they have certain expectations of us. These expectations are not the same. They misunderstand what we say, and we misunderstand what they do. There is nothing actually wrong with either of us—like those two people in the anecdote. Needing gas is legitimate, and wanting to help people is natural. But misunderstandings occur with fair frequency as the expectations fail to correlate.

There are many people who are not in church Sunday morning because they had entered there full of expectation, full of enthusiasm, full of hope a few months, weeks, or years ago. They said, "Meet my needs." And the church responded with a call to worship. In the misunderstanding that followed, they dropped out of the interaction. They were not willing to go through the process of misunderstanding to reach faith. What is the gospel—is it something to meet your needs, or something to equip you to meet the needs of others? If you come expecting one thing and get something else, you will quite naturally feel you have been shortchanged and misunderstood.

This theme of misunderstanding has a triple emphasis in chapter 12 of John, with the juxtaposed stories of Mary's anointing of Jesus, the high priests' death plot, and the great crowd's hosanna parade.

Anointing

The woman's extravagance was the first misunderstanding. While at dinner in the home of Lazarus and Mary and Martha, Mary took some costly perfume—the kind often used in anointing bodies for burial—and poured it over Jesus's feet. She then immediately wiped them with her hair. It was an act of extravagant devotion. Why did she do it? Clearly she thought Jesus was about to die. Rumors of death plots were in the air since Jesus raised Lazarus from the dead. That act had set in motion a conspiracy to put Jesus to death. Everyone close to Jesus would be aware of it. But there was more to it than that. Jesus had talked of his death, and the "in these last days" talk had increased. Jesus was going to die—that is the truth that Mary was acting upon. But she misunderstood the death. She assumed that it would be permanent.

And so her anticipatory embalming was evidence of her misunderstanding. Mary's response is typical—a misunderstanding that we can name "devotional pessimism." We see the loveliness of the gospel, and we realize the rarity of the words and presence of Jesus. Nothing else compares to it. But we know it is a lost cause. The forces of the world are too much, and we know our hopes will finally be dashed. The forces of the world are too much for it.

Religion for us then becomes an exercise in solemn nostalgia, and our faith is expressed as extravagant resignation. The best that the world has ever known is not going to survive in this cruel world. Evil is going to have the last word. There is no question of abandoning the cause. There is no crass expediency of trying at the last minute to shift sides so that we will be on the winning side. There is grief, and there is devotion. In Mary's anointing of Jesus, immense sadness and love were expressed in tears and devotion, for the love that came in Jesus would soon be gone. It was a lovely but futile life.

Jesus accepted the devotion. He did not reject it because it came in this misunderstanding. There was, after all, some truth in it. There would be a death. But the death was not, as Mary assumed, to be the last word. So Jesus accepted the outpouring of Mary's misunderstood love, but he didn't do what she expected him to do. The gospel would be able to absorb and assimilate all that devotion and lead into understanding by means of the Resurrection.

Day 28

Plotting

The second misunderstanding was with the Jewish leaders who were plotting to put Jesus to death. They understood that if Jesus were to be believed and followed, their leadership was doomed. The way of life they had promulgated, the power they had acquired, the authority they enjoyed—all that would be over. So they made a very logical response: they plotted to kill Jesus.

The conspiracy became elaborate. They developed a coalition conspiracy of Jewish leaders, Roman politicians, and the disciple Judas in order to get rid of the one who threatened what they counted of supreme value. They were quite correct at one level. They quite properly understood that Jesus's ways were in opposition to their own. They were alert in perceiving that what Jesus said would mean the end to what they were doing. Ambition would no longer be rewarded. Coercion would no longer be effective. Selfish lifestyles in which the strongest could work his will on the weak would become obsolete.

But they misunderstood. They did not realize they would be much happier without what they thought was important to them. They did not realize that a person is more whole when he shares his life than when he hoards it. They did not know that happiness and joy are a result of praising God, not being praised by men. They did not know any of these things—and they looked at the lordship of Christ only in terms of the disaster it would bring to their own positions of entrenched power.

Jesus accepted that misunderstanding. He did not reject what they were going to do to him. He could have, you know. He could have avoided the plots, exposed the conspiracy, and slipped from their clutches. But he let them do what they would. He absorbed the hate and rejection and went through with the Crucifixion. But he didn't stop there. He developed that rejection into acceptance. He turned that misunderstanding into an understanding that finds life in accepting God's will in Jesus Christ.

Day 29

Praise

The third misunderstanding took place in the crowd who paraded with Jesus into Jerusalem. They had a germ of understanding—that Jesus was king, that his lordship was good, and that his rule was to be desired. And so they greeted him with jubilation. They rallied around him in excited joy. So far, so good.

But they revealed their misunderstanding when they got branches and began to wave them in symbolic gestures expressing political, nationalistic hopes. The palm branch was a stereotypical symbol for political liberation. The crowd assumed that when Jesus went into Jerusalem, the Romans would be expelled, the occupying soldiers would be dispersed, and they would have a good Jewish king, like David, once more. They assumed there would be no more foreign domination and no more unfair taxation by the Gentiles.

Jesus silently protested that misunderstanding by getting a donkey and sitting on it as the parade progressed. This would remind the people that his rule was a rule of peace (expressed by the donkey), not a rule of military might (for which the symbol was the prancing warhorse). But the people didn't seem to notice at the time. They were too excited by what they saw as the imminent fulfillment of their dreams.

This is a wish-fulfillment misunderstanding. The people had

strong wishes that they had dreamed about. They hoped that Jesus might fulfill them. There seemed to be good reason that he might—he did talk of providing for all our needs, he did show that he was able to make men whole, to provide whatever they need for a complete, eternal life. The misunderstanding came because they were caught up with their own wish-fulfillment fantasies and were paying very little attention to the reality of Jesus's actions and words.

But again, Jesus did not get angry at their misunderstanding. He accepted their applause, and he rode in their parade. But he didn't stop there. He assimilated their enthusiasm and their expectation into his ministry. Then he offered it back to them in the Resurrection, which would fulfill needs and desires and wishes that they never even knew they had.

So you see our misunderstandings—from whatever base they have their origin, from our courageous realism, our selfish defensiveness, our fantasies of wish fulfillments—are accepted and absorbed in Jesus and brought to wholeness. It doesn't finally matter that we come to church on Sundays for the wrong reason—out of a sense of nostalgia or out of a childish sense that it might bring us luck. It does not finally matter that some are even now trying to find ways to avoid the demands of Christ, to get rid of the claims of his lordship, to protectively try to preserve what we pitifully call "our right." The gospel is not ruined by our misunderstandings. Jesus takes the reality in our misconceptions—the reality of death, the reality of repentance, the reality of lordship—and through the process of the Passion and Crucifixion and Resurrection, he makes a whole gospel out of it. He leads us along the path of discipleship, in which we learn to find that we are sharing his love and a life that is eternal.

Isn't that good news? That our misunderstandings, no matter how well intentioned or how badly intentioned, do not disqualify us from being part of the movement of people who experience resurrection and who by faith participate in the saving love of Jesus Christ? No matter what you came full of today—full of forebodings, full of resistance, full of illusions—the more important reality is that Jesus is here. And our fragmentary misunderstandings hold no candle to his comprehensive understanding and love of us.

Amen.

Words

When he comes, he'll expose the error of the godless
world's view of sin, righteousness, and judgment: He'll
show them that their refusal to believe in me is their
basic sin; that righteousness comes from above, where
I am with the Father, out of their sight and control;
that judgment takes place as the ruler of this godless
world is brought to trial and convicted.

JOHN 16:8–11

In recent years there have been several books and innumerable magazine articles on the subject of increasing one's vocabulary. Educational research has found that there is a close relationship between a person's vocabulary and his or her IQ. The Human Engineering Laboratory, a New York institution that tests people's aptitudes, has found that the only common characteristic of successful people in this country is an unusual grasp of the meaning of words.

Religious vocabulary is a common place for floundering, misstating, and misunderstanding. As we deal with the important world of eternal relationships, it is particularly important that we get our words right. Jesus knew this and told his disciples just before his crucifixion and resurrection that one of the primary functions of his risen presence among them would be to sharpen their vocabularies and put new meanings into old words so that they would be capable of thinking and talking clearly about themselves and God.

When it comes to today's passage, it's helpful to look at a few different translations of John 16:8:

"When he is come, he will reprove the world of sin, and of righteousness, and of judgment" (KJV).

"When he comes, he will convince the world concerning sin and righteousness and judgment" (RSV).

"When he comes, he will confute the world, and show them where wrong and right and judgment lie" (NEB).

Three different translations use three different words to describe what Jesus will do—*reprove, convince,* and *confute.* The Greek word behind the English translations means "to bring to the light, to expose." The NEB uses two words to bring out the full meaning: *confute* and *show. Confute* means "to bring overwhelming evidence in order to disprove a position," while *show* indicates the positive evidence for the new position. The KJV *reprove* and the RSV *convince* combine these ideas, as they are in the Greek word, and we see both the positive and the negative directions of the word. As our Lord works with us on our vocabularies, he exposes our wrong usages and then convinces us to the right usage. He *confutes* and *shows.*

Sin. It is a difficult word to get to the core of. It is so overgrown with secondary meaning, so encrusted with sloppy usage, and so prone to become the private word of both the sincere and the unscrupulous that if there is any word in the world on which we need help, it is this one. We need to be confuted, and we need to be shown. We need to see it exposed in all of its wrong usage. We need to see what it really is.

The meaning of sin is connected with the refusal to believe in

Jesus Christ: "He will convict them of wrong by their refusal to believe in me." Jesus Christ is the representative of the fullness of God in the world. He is the point of exposition of the nature of God. Where Jesus is, God is. A refusal to believe in Jesus Christ is a refusal to believe in God's presence in human history. Sin is the rejection of that presence—a refusal to act as if God did in fact invade our lives. Sin is not atheism. All the best sinners believe in God, but they just don't connect him with anything that is alive and vital in their lives.

Paul equated sin with falling "short of the glory of God" (Romans 3:23). In other words, "everything which is other than God would have it be is sin."* God wills life and love. Sin is an avoidance of that, a denial and rejection of it. Sin is always, therefore, less than life and an amputation and attenuation of the vital.

G. K. Chesterton's Father Brown in one place said, "My chief complaint against sin is that it is so boring." When you refuse the core meaning of life, taking away the living part of existence, it cannot help but be boring, dull, and monotonous. Sin is life pursuing death. And that, I suppose, is why sin has to advertise itself so frantically. We need to be told over and over again how much fun it is, how enjoyable it is, and how much happiness it will bring us. In itself, sin carries none of that conviction, so it is always dependent

---

* William Temple, *Fellowship with God* (London: Macmillan, 1920), 95.

on a vigorous press agency to persuade us. Righteousness needs none of that advertising. So we have a world that is full of talk on how exciting sin is and nearly silent about righteousness.

Sin is not primarily a matter of morality but a matter of a certain kind of living. Morality has something to do with this living but only subordinately. Life is the concern of the Scriptures and of the Christian church. And because some things are open threats to life, they are labeled sins. But at its center, sin is the rejection of the presence of God in our lives. God is the source of life, and if we reject that life, we have cut off our source. We diminish in our joy like a river whose source has dried up.

More Words

Righteousness. "When he comes, he will convince the world concerning sin and righteousness and judgment" (John 16:8). The meaning of *righteousness* has something to do with the absence of Jesus. He leaves so that the disciples are no longer able to see him, and thereby they are shown what righteousness means.

The idea confuted here is that right is visible and apparent. We commonly identify righteousness with successfulness. We admire the winner in athletics, the rich person in business, and the honor student in academics. That which is on top is the best—the right. Sometimes that identification is correct, but sometimes it is not. And the reason for this inconsistency is that right derives its meaning from something else—a relationship with God. And that relationship is not visible: "You will see me no more" (verse 10). The righteousness Christ shows is unrelated to appearances. He was crucified at a young age, which seemed to show that his kingdom was a failure and his program would dissolve. But the Resurrection gave the disciples irrefutable evidence that he was with the Father and that he was right. Righteousness is a quality derivative from a divine relationship unseen to the unbelieving eye.

Recently I was shown a book authored by a man I know fairly well. The man is garrulous, apparently unlettered, and rustic. He talks with a prominent Swedish accent, passes the time of day with anyone on the street, and reveals no marks of culture or sophistication. The book is on the growth and care of trees. And this man is the author. It has been through six editions, the last one two years ago. It is packed with Latin phrases, compendious in its information, and used as a textbook in many forestry classes at university schools. The relation between appearance and knowledge in that man was (to me) invisible. Jesus's point about righteousness is similar. What looks like righteousness often is not. Righteousness is based on the invisible: the relationship of Jesus to his Father, and the relationship between man and God. What looks in this world like failure and muddling is actually eternally successful, that is, righteous.

Judgment. Last but not least. Like the other words, this one is defined in relationship to the person of Jesus Christ. The common usage refers to the objective and the future. It is often accompanied by the prospect of punishments or rewards. A judge makes a judgment on a person and either acquits or sentences him. A judge in a track meet judges a winner and gives him or her a medal. This word is nearly always used in the final future sense—it comes at the end of an action or performance.

In religion, we use it that way too. There will be a day of judgment when the good and the bad are sorted out. This will all take place either when we die or at some future date in eternity when the end of the world has come and everyone is called up in a great company for the final reckoning. Now, Jesus didn't completely throw this idea out the window, but he did rearrange it considerably. He said we would know the meaning of divine judgment because "the ruler of this world is judged" (verse 11). The disciples saw this at the time of the Crucifixion. Jesus was before Pilate in a legal court of law. But Jesus said that it was Pilate that was judged, not himself—Pilate was a representative of the "ruler of this world." In any confrontation with Jesus Christ, it is not God on trial, but us. Judgment is not a decision we make but a disposition that is made of us by our own reaction to him.

The so-called "last judgment" or "final judgment" will make plain—publicly displaying—these judgments that have been working internally in the lives of each person all along. Life is a single package. We do not live one part of life now and get our rewards and punishments later on. Eternity breaks in now. Judgment takes place daily. Sin is the daily killing of life, and righteousness is a daily resurrection into the presence of God. Judgment has already taken place, and the ruler of this world has already been judged.

Words such as *sin* and *righteousness* and *judgment* must be won back to the meaning that Christ gave them. They have to be defined in the presence of the living God. They have their existence only as they reflect some part of Jesus Christ, who is God with us. In every case, these words receive their meanings as they tell of a part of Christ's life. The risen Christ meets us, and as he does he confutes the world in its use of these old words and then goes on to show where wrong and right and judgment really lie. Amen.

THE DEFINITIVE COLLECTION
of
EUGENE PETERSON'S
TEACHINGS

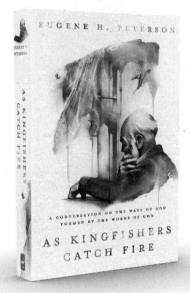

As Kingfishers Catch Fire draws you closer to the Christ "who lives and acts in us in such ways that our lives express the congruence of inside and outside…so that we find ourselves living, almost in spite of ourselves, the Christ life in the Christ way."

Through the life and words of Eugene Peterson, you'll discover why each of us is called to be a friend to God.

Learn more at
WaterBrookMultnomah.com